G000113035

MY JOURNEY

WITH A

REMARKABLE TREE

Ken Finn

Published by Eye Books

Edited by Chris Davison

My Journey with a Remarkable Tree
1st Edition
March 2005

Published by Eye Books Ltd
51 Boscombe Rd
London
W12 9HT
Tel/fax: +44 (0) 20 8743 3276
website: www.eye-books.com

Set in Frutiger and Garamond
ISBN: 1903070368

British Library Cataloguing in Publication Data
A catalogue record for this book is available from the British Library

Printed and bound in Great Britain by Biddles Ltd
Printed on FSC certified Munken Paper from Arctic Paper - supplied by Denmaur

CONTENTS

FOREWORD

ACKNOWLEDGEMENTS

SECTION ONE - MEETING WITH A GURU
1 KAURI MORNING   2
2 BISTO COUNTRY   3

SECTION TWO - NINETEEN
3 DOWN IN PHNOM PENH   6
4 YOU SHOULD KNOW   9
5 FINDING A GUIDE   13

SECTION THREE - TO THE TEMPLE
6 ROAD TO RUINS   18
7 NO GOOD GUYS   26
8 ALIEN RUMBLE   30
9 TEMPLE SUBTERFUGE   34
10 BACK TO CHUCKS   39
11 BADLANDS   42
12 SHARK SOUP   49
13 ANGKOR SUNRISE   53
14 ANGKOR TWILIGHT   58

SECTION FOUR - EDUCATING RITA
15 FAST TRACK   62
16 RITA   65
17 A NEW GUIDE   68

SECTION FIVE - NO TREES NO RAIN
18 THE ROAD TO TUM RING   72
19 INTO THE FOREST   76
20 NO SHIT   81

21 TOP RANKIN TUM RING   86
22 TAR KONG   88
23 PISSON GOD   91
24 DESPERATELY SPEAKING ENGLISH   97
25 THUNDER   102
26 MISS U SCARECROW   103

SECTION SIX - EDUCATING RITA PART TWO
27 SLUETH IN PP   106
28 PART P.PEOPLE   111

SECTION SEVEN - GREEN GEM
29 PATCHES   116
30 KACHUN   119
31 SLASH N SAVE   123
32 SPIRIT LIGHTS   127
33 LOW TAR   130
34 OILED   135
35 GREEN RAT STEW   139
36 PANT BOYS   143
37 GRUB N GRAB   146
38 CHAMAU   149

SECTION EIGHT - PILGRIMS PROGRESS
39 FREEDOM TRAIL   152
40 BILLY NO MATES   156
41 NO FSC IN VN   160
42 LOVE AND MDF   165
43 HEAVENS ABOVE   168
44 HEAVENS RIGHT HERE   173
45 WING ANA HOPE   177
46 MENTAL DADIO   181
47 HOLE IN THE WALL   184

48 Mr Nasty   189
49 No Baps   193
50 Little Hands   196
51 Tree in a Basket   200

Section Nine - Don't Buy It
52 Don't Buy It   208

Section Ten - Outta Here
53 Out of Juice   212
54 Strange Fish   215

Section Eleven - Krime And Meanie
55 Part 1. A Scary Tale   220
56 Part 2. Dead Enders   224
57 Rich Country Poor People   229

Section Twelve - Blighty
58 Ming and Von   234
59 Mssrs 20 Percent   239

Epilogue   243

Foreword

In the lowland rainforests of south-east Asia, from India to Vietnam and down the Malay peninsula, there grows a tall and stately old-growth tree called Dipterocarpus alatus, otherwise known as the hairy-leafed apitong or 'Chhoeuteal'. In Cambodia, where it is locally preserved as a votive, spirit tree, forest-dwellers tap its trunk for resin during the dry season – collecting up to 40 gallons from a single tree – to use for lighting their homes and waterproofing their boats, or as a cash-crop ingredient for varnishes and paints.

The World Conservation Union lists the Chhoeuteal's status as EN: endangered. Not by the locals who love and understand it, who hardly ever cut one down; but by Asian timber companies and manufacturers, many of them corrupt, who cannot get enough of its magnificent, dark-red, weather-resistant hardwood timber, known as keruing, made into garden furniture and exported to the west by the container-load. You can see examples at your local garden centre.

This is the story of one of those groves of trees (illegally cut down in Cambodia, smuggled across the border into Vietnam, laundered into sustainably-sourced artefacts, exported in a container to Felixstowe); and of their pursuit by a brave and passionate man, the author of this book. His story is all the more shocking for its focus: a paradigm of what is happening all over the world, in the Brazilian rainforest, in the Russian taiga, among the giant eucalypts of Tasmania, in the temperate rainforest of the Canadian Great Bear. In the last half-century Cambodia has lost a third of its old-growth forest-cover, devastated by war, logging and conversion to monocultural, MDF-making species like acacia and eucalyptus. A greater area has been degraded by the removal of the choicest trees, and that very degradation is often used as an excuse for total annihilation. But local villagers argue that if the land is left alone for 15 or 20 years, the big trees will grow again. "If they destroy the old forest they might as well come to kill us all. It is our rice pot."

Jonathan Roberts
author - Mythic Woods - The Worlds Most Remarkable Forest

Acknowledgements

Somehow "My Journey with a Remarkable Tree" has had an energy of its own from the day I decided to take to its road. Maybe fate or some other hidden process was at work but I have never felt that this was my project alone. Kismet has done wonderful service in steering me to the resources I have needed or in creating meetings that at times have seemed spookily pertinent. I'm sincerely grateful.

Fated or not I'm thankful for the help I received both in Cambodia and Vietnam as well as back home in England. I would like to thank my guides and in particular Sena and his family for their hospitality. A big one to Global Witness for their assistance and for the work they undertake in countries like Cambodia; for highlighting the corruption that creates poverty in a land rich in resources. Thanks go to WildAid who acted on my evidence of wildlife trading in Preah Vear and for all those who helped me along the way. Probably more importantly my gratitude goes to those who are working still to protect the forest.

Back in the UK I would like to thank my Editor Chris Davison for his clarity and my publisher Dan for his support and understanding. That this book is printed on Forest Stewardship Council (FSC) paper is a credit to Eye Books for going the extra mile both in terms of effort and expense. It couldn't have been anything but 100% Recycled or FSC certified paper for me but as it turns out going 'Ancient Forest Friendly' was actually something quite ground breaking in book publishing. The paper used is a minimum 30% certified content and I have been assured that the remainder is according to FSC 'from forests that are not illegally logged and where workers rights are respected, not genetically modified and neither from high conservation forest or from areas where there are extant social disputes regarding the forest.' We hope that as more publishers and authors begin to insist on recycled or truly sustainable virgin pulp papers like FSC this process will get easier and more economically viable. If you enjoy reading my book please share it with someone else or give it to a charity shop or library. Share more, buy less.

Finally I would like to dedicate this book to my partner who has supported me through the process and a big loving hug to my sons, grandchildren, family and friends.

MEETING WITH A GURU

Do you believe in spirits? After my

encounter with the 'Lord of the Forest'

I'm a believer. In the forests of Northland

New Zealand there live today giant

Kauri trees over two thousand years

old. My unexpected and otherworldly

connection with one was the start of an

incredible journey.

1 Kauri Morning

Dressed like a castaway in the presence of the Lord of the Forest, 'Te Matua Ngahere', I'm the fan singled out to have my hand shaken, the child with the posy for the king or the believer receiving the blessing. The heavy pitter-patter of rainfall on my shroud of yellow plastic is an anchor to the world I know back there but right here right now I'm wired to a force of wisdom two thousand years old. In the quiet pounding of my brain the tumblers whir to find a combination that makes sense, yet somewhere else in my being where electricity plays no part, a light of understanding is flowing perfectly clear; release, everything, stillness.

My audience is over and I stand nodding, smiling and tearful. Grateful. I've found my guru.

Tingling at every nerve ending I walk back to this world but the after glow is confirmation if any was needed that something very profound has happened to me. Every colour is richer, sound clearer and sensation more intense. I'm in love. Not for the love of someone or something but immersed in love.

2 Bisto Country

It had been the wettest summer month of February on record, New Zealand's treasures had been snatched between the storms and showers but today there was no respite. We sloshed into the forest leaving my sisters, 'the golden girls' dry but steamed up in the car. This morning we were a couple of 'see it and run' day-trippers in plastic macs, Brits used to making the most of it.

Bunty and I followed the timber walkway around the museum of trees to the 'Four Sisters' a cluster of Giant Kauri that closed the canopy above us. We gawped up while lashings of fresh rain filled our hoods and faces before squelching on to 'Te Matua Ngahere' The Lord of the Forest. Like a pair of giggling kids tumbling into a cathedral we were suddenly aware of its majesty. There he stood over two thousand years old, as wide as a house towering up to the heavens, an ancient monument of living timber. At least thirty generations of man including Christ have lived and died during his lifetime. I was mesmerised

For a while I was lost in what I can only describe as a silent dialogue with a tree. I was drawn in and somehow connected to its pure wisdom for a timeless moment. I experienced no internal speech or reasoning I was taken straight to the point of understanding or recognition. The clarity blew me away.

On the way back to the car my senses heightened as if tripping on a beautiful substance I enjoyed the freshness of the forest its intense colours and a physical lightness. It was more than just a hedonistic rush; something deep inside me had taken a jolt.

I wanted to stay in the moment; clarity can be lost in an instant. Life like a fog will roll in and blunt the edges of certainty but we were back at the car and I had to give up something to return to normality. I was high on the experience but I knew that I would sound scary if I just recounted what had happened to me. I had to try and put it in an acceptable form. I was as honest as I could be and told everyone I'd just had a special connection with the Giant Kauri.

A family wedding brought us to the country that's lived in my mind through the glossy calendars and mementos my big sister sent back every year since I was small child. Since I waved goodbye to a small face and flapping handkerchief at the rail atop the towering Ocean Liner off to a big country of mountains, forests and Maoris. She left behind a late 50's England I remember without colour emigrating with the thousands of other hopefuls looking for a bright new future in the sun.

Over time the big country in Technicolor seemed to me to become smaller and smaller and I became fearful of an encounter with the claustrophobic British home from home with its exotic lodgers. But here we were five brothers and sisters all together for the first time in twenty years and it was great. God's own country as they used to call it was still very much of my imaginings, a green and pleasant land with Bisto on the breeze but now more cosy than small and I'm happy to have witnessed it.

At our farewell party my brother-in-law said, "I hear you had an experience with one of our Kauri trees." Careful not to sound like an old hippy I told him that I had felt a strong connection. "Ah yes, there's an old tradition among bushmen here that if you're feeling tired the best thing you can do is to hug a big tree. It recharges your energy." It was the comment, the small seed from which my journey grew.

Bunty my partner was heading to India for nearly two months to train as a yoga teacher. I had a stopover on the way back to the UK in hand and now a plan was beginning to take shape in my mind. The experience with the Giant Kauri had really moved me yet already the clarity of the moment was beginning to be lost. During a trip to Cambodia a couple of years previous I'd heard a few tantalising stories about the 'Spirit Trees' that live in the forest there. A return trip seemed to be the perfect opportunity to go in search of a big recharge and new enlightenment. I imagined going well beyond the beaten track to find more powerful trees and to encounter people who regularly commune with them; to cement in my mind the wisdom passed on by the Kauri.

NINETEEN

In 1975 Pol Pot and the Khmer Rouge

reset the clock to year zero. Had his

lunatic scheme succeeded Cambodia or

Kampuchea as he named it would be

just nineteen. Its a teenager shaped by

very troubled times. You'd be wise to be

mindful of its dark side but all the more

amazed by its optimism and joy.

3 Down in Phnom Penh

The atmosphere over Phnom Penh was lumpy and my flight bumped and rolled downward. A collection of western browns and blondes swayed above the rows of shiny black Asian haircuts that jiggled in rows just visible over their seatbacks. The landscape below was dry and parched, flat and brown to the horizon, it was so different from my last visit, then the paddies were an intense green. With a bash and a squeak we were on the runway. The engines were still in reverse thrust and the pilot was breaking hard but the clink of buckles unclipping was to be heard all round the cabin, I made the decision not to get involved in the free for all.

I'm the accidental traveller. Over the years I've amassed a collection of what Bunty calls "Kenny stories." Mishaps, misunderstandings and missed departures. I promised her that on this trip I was going to be sorted, a bit more focused but I failed on the first hurdle. I'd left all my cash in the 'hold' luggage and had no way of paying for my visa on arrival. Expecting a bureaucratic hassle I went into a small pleading amateur dramatic, however the very pleasant immigration lady waved this aside and took me beyond the passport desk to  get my bag and $20. I was happily waiting for my stamp when the guy next to me opened a conversation with a little rant about the 'fuckin rip off' visa fee and went straight into his life story – a hard time tale of taxi driving in Birmingham and a broken marriage.

Somehow he was looking for a new start, hoping to 'make a bit' with his guitar. With a small shudder I imagined being stuck in cab with this 'Brummy Leonard Cohen' and immediately realised the benefits of the motorcycle taxi but then maybe Phnom Penh would give him a bigger view on life. With a lighter heart I imagined him giving music lessons to street kids.

I'd been here before and any traveller will recognise the joy of knowing the ropes on arrival and I was pleased to be away from the terminal in quick time, dodging the sharksters and chancers. The $2 moto ride into town took about 20 minutes, and my ability to roughly navigate to my destination afforded me a little bit of 'local' status. I secured a nice room in a mid range place favoured by NGO workers; it had a few solid pieces of furniture, a big old fridge, a desk and view of the street.

It was Sunday and I cheerfully spend the afternoon wandering around and revisiting favourite places. I walked out past the Independence Monument and children playing in the spray of the fountains nearby and down to the riverfront. Once a shabby old market strip the area was cleared five years or so ago and an open space created with an embankment wall and ornamental lights, wide pavement and grassed gardens. It still looked a bit new but it was busy with locals and westerners mingling together in a slightly hectic promenade. Young jobbing photographers offered to snap and sell photos to their punters on big old iconic Nikons and Cannons that fifteen years ago would have been slung round the necks of photojournalists. Now there was a 'Kiss me Quick' atmosphere about the place; couples canoodled on the wall while children played ball and flew kites, vendors sold lurid coloured drinks, barbecued fish, meats and an array of plastic trinkets. It was easy to just wander and take in the sights and smells.

I strolled along behind couple of young Western guys wearing scruffy fashionable anti-fashion grunge - torn and modified work wear, unlaced boots and faded slogan T-shirts. It's a tribal statement clearly understood by disaffected western youth and anyone on the protest frontline. Here though I watched the puzzled looks of the locals. I wondered about their thought processes and how I might explain to a poor Cambodian trying to earn enough to be rid of the

7

look of the dirty street how this fashion statement worked.

A stiff and sudden afternoon breeze from the river whipped along the grills of the searing food and bundled the thick blue smoke into a wayward balloon. It billowed across the main road and into the open fronted restaurants and colonial balconies of the affluent before funnelling down a side street. The road was packed with the Sunday afternoon "Darling" a motorised promenade of bikes and cars; everyone in their best outfits, dressed to be seen. A horde of little Honda step-through's choked the road and the combined exhaust note created a rumble that drowned out the beeps of the flashy Landcruisers caught like beetles in an ant trail. I surrendered to the lures of a Gin and Tonic at the Foreign Correspondents bar on the other side of the 'Darling'. Showing off, I crossed the road using the 'Saigon Technique', which is to walk into the road slowly and deliberately and allow the traffic to avoid you. It takes a bit of balls the first time, to just launch yourself into a wall of traffic but as long as you move predictably it works.

The FCC balcony is a favourite spot for Expats and tourists to watch the world go by, it's a safe haven. Looking out beyond the road and the wide strip of municipal grass the big brown Tonle Sap River flows past on its way down to meet up with the Mekong. The last time I was here it flowed in the opposite direction; when the monsoon rains deluge the Mekong the river acts as a big drain filling the huge Tonle Sap Lake up stream. But little else has changed and I'm glad to be back.

4 You Should Know

I'm surprised by how many people in 2004 are only vaguely aware of Pol Pot and the Khmer Rouge. These days Cambodia is ranked as one of the older 21st century post conflict countries; a first step on the ladder for career NGO or Donor organisation personnel. Cambodia's past has been overshadowed by more current atrocities, wars and crusades but it's a history worth looking at as it illuminates all to well history repeating itself. If you know the story you can skip a bit and if you're interested in reading more, I'll suggest a couple of great books. I have to tell you about what happened here because it makes the beautiful Cambodian smile all the more remarkable. With a few apologies to the serious historians of S.E. Asia, here's my potted version of the last forty years or so for those less academically minded.

The French abandon Vietnam and Indochina after a thorough kicking by Uncle Ho Chi Minh and his communist fighters at Diem Binh Phu. The country is temporarily divided into two pending an election and the combatants are told to go to their rooms, the miserable Viet Cong to the North and the happy Capitalists to the South. Uncle Ho looks set to win the ballot and Ngo Dinh Diem, our man in Saigon bottles out on the National elections. Instead he calls a referendum on his continued rule of the South and wins comfortably despite getting more votes than voters. With China and Russia chucking its weight behind their boy Ho Chi Minh in Hanoi and the USA pumping cash and arms in to shore up the South the classic standoff develops.

With a big guy to back him up and the money rolling in Diem starts to throw his weight around and generally act the tyrant. His popularity plummets – monks are setting light to themselves at parties thrown in his honour. Maybe it was time to do a deal with Uncle Ho up North. Wrong! The US supports a coup and Diem gets a bullet in the head. A new hardliner brings only temporary respite on a downward spiral. The South Vietnamese army are deserting in droves, up to 2000 men a month when the brass start to think about throwing it in for a fast boat out. With an investment to protect and sixteen thousand 'advisers' already in the country the USA decides to seriously join the fray. Blaming Uncle Ho and to justify its direct military involvement, the US fabricate an attack on two of their warships in the Bay of Tonkin. American politicians; and this has become a habit for them, put together a small allegiance of the willing; the Australians, New Zealanders, South Koreans, The Philippines and Thai's to gain wider international support for the venture. By 1969 there are half a million Americans and allies fighting and dying in Vietnam. As the conflict drags on and the casualties grow the US forces with various partners secretly enlarge the war across the Vietnamese border into neighbouring Laos and Cambodia, carpet-bombing and killing thousands of people they have treaties of peace with. It must be acknowledged that they're out to crush the North Vietnamese who are also trampling over peace accords here but by the end of the war Laos holds the dubious record of the 'most bombed country in history'. The bombing and covert operations on the ground are the military machine's little secret; one it can't ask congress to bankroll so the CIA allegedly finances the whole scheme with drugs money! The Golden Triangle countries whose opium production has fallen into disrepair are built up to provide

a chunky revenue stream and in turn to feed the addiction of G.I. junkies fighting the war on the ground. By 1973 the Americans have had enough and ship out. This humiliation is to colour their  involvement in the region for a long time. Before regret becomes the dominant sentiment the US and its allies continue to meddle, to withhold aid and effectively create an atmosphere where anarchy, corruption and the rule of the gun flourishes.

The American bombing and a subsequent land invasion of Cambodia in pursuit of the Viet Cong has a huge effect upon the stability of the country and sets the stage for one of the most extreme experiments of social engineering in history, 'Year Zero'. Taking advantage of the turmoil created by these events the revolutionary government of the Khmer Rouge lead by the dark figure of Pol Pot comes to power in 1975. Within two weeks of its victorious entry into Phnom Penh the entire population is emptied into the countryside and the process of turning the country into a Maoist, agrarian peasantry begins. Connection with the outside world is severed, currency abolished, postal services closed down and an ancient history wiped away with the date reset to Zero. The middle classes; teachers, doctors, lecturers anyone with an education are sent for re-education and later extermination; wearing glasses is a pointer to an education and a death sentence. The masses are grouped into 'work parties' to carry out large agricultural projects but because of widespread organisational failure famine spreads. They die in droves. As the experiment spirals out of control the Party becomes increasingly paranoid and seeks to purge itself from within and former comrade kills comrade. Innocence is brutalised as children are trained to become the guards of revolution and in turn reveal the brutal nature of our species; 'The Killing Fields' are a testament to the barbarism. As Year Zero clicks one through four over two million people have been killed under the vicious regime.

There's another twenty years of lies, corruption and double-dealing and even a cameo performance by the British SAS to train The Khmer Rouge in ever more sophisticated ways of death but I'm sure you get the picture.

One thing I can't help but wonder is where did all this get anyone apart from misery? By my reckoning, adding up the various historical accounts, the Vietnam War and the associated wars it spawned in Cambodia and Laos killed upwards of five million people and yet the political landscape remains largely unchanged. Lives and nature wrecked with good money pissed down the drain for what? If you're up for it I would read "First

They Killed My Father", by Loung Ung, a harrowing account of a child's survival and "Voices from S21" by David Chandler. In a suburb of Phnom Penh the Khmer Rouge turned a High School into a high security prison, S21, where they systematically tortured inmates before sending them to their deaths. None of it for the squeamish but you should know.

And so back to the Cambodian smile. I have been moved to tears by the intensity of a Cambodian smile. The blank face that is somewhere else, busy perhaps or maybe a hint of worry but then it catches you watching and crinkles into a delicious chocolate wrapper of a grin. And when you smile back it just keeps on going until you think it can't get any bigger. And there you are beaming at each other, it's beautiful but you'd easily be mistaken for 'Care in the Community' in Britain.

5 Finding a Guide

I'd made the decision to avoid the regular backpackers places and trails but without the ubiquitous 'Lonely Planet' to rely on I needed a guide to show me beyond the well-trodden road. Fortunately I found myself amongst a rich alternative source of knowledge. My hotel was just down the road from the United Nations and in the surrounding streets was a community of Non Governmental Organisations (NGOs), charities and campaign groups. The hotel lobby and restaurants were busy with western personnel; outside their Landcruisers vied for kerb space. Over coffee I talked about what I was trying to do with a couple of guys who worked for an Environmental Agency, I wanted to find the Spirit Forests I'd heard about the last time I was here. They gave me the number of a Khmer (Cambodian) guide who they used from time to time. He was up North somewhere showing some Japanese aid workers around and wouldn't be back for a couple of days. They suggested in the meantime I should visit some of the Charities and Aid Agencies to find a different view on the country. The UN Library was a good place to start.

I'd imagined that the hallowed ground of the UN would be foreboding but the guard on the gate gave me a pass and showed me in with little more than a look. Somehow I felt a bit of a fraud but I told the librarian that I was researching ethnic minorities and spiritual beliefs. He smiled and helpfully pulled out some titles then left me to it. There was some great stuff; too much for one sitting. I noticed references to the 'Forest Network' a collective of NGOs and charities working with forest issues and indigenous peoples. The librarian gave me its address and I headed off on a moto see if there was anyone to talk to.

Arriving on the cusp of lunchtime every body was either gone or going. The receptionist said the 'Forest Network' people were out on fieldwork but I could take a look at their publication list to see if there was anything of interest. I did a quick search on the library PC and it brought up a list that included a book on

'Spirit Forests'. It was a start but searching the shelves it wasn't to be found. The lady with the keys just wanted to lock up and take her lunch and I had let go for now but the information was waiting for me to find it.

Later that evening I spoke to the guide on his mobile, Kim Kong, great name I thought. He said he would be happy to guide me and we made an appointment to meet as soon as he got back. I put the fact that I couldn't really understand him that well down to the crap reception on his cell phone.

Over the next couple of days I biked about town going to different offices and agencies researching destinations and having fun going places other travellers didn't go. The one reference to Spirit Trees was all I had come up with so far but I reckoned that once I found a guide I'd get the information I wanted. I was beginning to see a much bigger picture of Cambodia in the sheer number of projects and issues being addressed by foreign NGOs and charities. I was beginning to wonder if I could do something constructive with my time here once I'd found my Spirit Trees.

At the hotel I got a call from reception to say that Kim Kong was waiting to see me. I was dead keen but wanted to be cool, we had a deal to strike before heading off into the wilds. As Kim shook my hand he was clearly talking to me but for the life of me I couldn't make it out. I kept shaking in the hope that it would become clear but it sounded like a mouthful of tofu. Now we were shaking hands well beyond the cultural norm though Kim obviously thought this was a custom he hadn't encountered before and kept shaking and smiling. I panicked and became fixed upon his safari suit - beige Crimplene, as crisp as the day it left the ICI factory in 1973 I imagined. My feet were already making escape plans when thankfully something turned the big knob on my mental Star Trek interpreter and I got the gist of what he was saying. We broke contact and sat down. It wasn't a good start and I found it hard to stay on the correct channel but in between the tofu I heard him say, "$100 a day and not for another ten day." I was gutted, I'd waited around for pretty much a week already and $100 a day was way over my budget. I had hoped that I would find a guide who might be closer to people and nature but Kim's ego was as loud as his suit. I voluntarily switched my interpreter back to tofu while he waved his arms in big expansive sweeps. The excitement of arranging a new adventure slipped away.

Despondent I skulked about over the weekend but on Monday I met the guys who'd recommended Kim Kong. They were sorry to hear that things hadn't worked out with him. In connection with the Spirit Forests they suggested a few more sources including the Forest Network. A Cambodian colleague of theirs who'd hardly said a word joined the conversation to tell me more. He introduced himself as Sena, and he told me he'd interviewed an old guy who knew all about the spirits and ceremony. He had some great recordings that he'd play me sometime. It was clear he knew something of the Spirit Trees and of the beliefs too. He told me that the spirits lived in all things, water and stones and how some trees hid and of rocks that made you sleep. Each had its own character. As he talked I began to add detail to my ideal of a spirit forest. I visualised the pure light breaking through the canopy a hundred feet above me. Standing amongst giants and bathing in the vital energy of a forest pristine and vibrant green. Somehow it would be returning to my childhood wonder of the woods. As we talked it was clear that we had made a connection and that my enthusiasm about spirit trees had touched him. I thought to myself it would be great if I had this guy as my guide but out loud I bemoaned the fact that I was still languishing in the Capital. I hoped he might pick up on the unsaid. Sena looked at me hard for a moment and then said, "I'm going on a field trip tomorrow, maybe you want to come with me? I can show you a Spirit Tree on the way." Then looked to his colleagues for a confirmation this was OK. They nodded an 'all right then' as if we were a couple of kids 'pretty pleasing' for a sleep over. Then to check he said, "I'm leaving at 6 o'clock in the morning and we'll be travelling by moto. It will be hard, are you sure? We're going to the Preah Vear Temple. It'll take three days." "Sure", I said not knowing where the Preah Vear Temple was, but I could have kissed him.

TO THE TEMPLE

Prassat Preah Veah is set high in the

rugged country that divides Cambodia

and Thailand. The well off neighbour

has provided tarmac comfort right to

the steps on its side of the mountain.

Our journey is on one of the hardest

roads in Cambodia.

6 The Road to Ruins

Sena had said to meet him at six. I sat enthusiastically early on a step at the corner of the road watching the motos dodging the white joggers and dog walkers; the NGO industry limbering up before the heat of the day.

Preceded by a glorious aroma that kicked off my stomach juices, a street food vendor trundled by with her little café on a barrow. I jumped up and stopped her. The wok was steaming with vegetable noodles and it all looked beautifully fresh. I gestured, yes please, she gestured to meat; I shook no, she held up an egg with a grin and I nodded yes. With a few waves at the hot charcoal with a bit of board the egg was sizzling under the noodles and in moments dished up on a china plate with a handful of fresh herbs on top. Deelish.

A scruffy Khmer stopped on a beat up old motorbike and smiled, clearly he knew me. I did a double take and realised it was Sena – he'd certainly dressed down. He squatted beside me and lit up a cigarette, he had a few things to say before we set off. " I'm going to take a look at

the route up to Preah Vear for the agency. If anyone asks, you're my friend and we're going up to the temple together, I'm your guide. OK?" "Sure", I said. He half frowned, half smiled; "It'll be a hard ride." "I'll be OK", I said beginning to wonder a little. The enthusiasm was strong though and we headed off.

Sena said he'd arranged a couple of trusted moto riders in Kompon Thom; about three hours North of Phnom Penh and we made our way there in a shared taxi, three in the front, four in the back. It was a fairly smooth tarmac road and I watched the scenery while he joked and laughed with everyone. He was definitely a bit of a chameleon, yesterday he had sat quietly sizing me up, cards close to his chest but today in the cab he was larging it up. He had everyone involved.

At the bus station, Ret and Rat, our riders for the next three-days emerged from the throng. They looked a bit down at heel but cheerful and I guessed happy with the prospect of a few days solid employment. Rat's bike was really worse for wear and he probably carried the large stirrup pump to sustain the flaccid looking tyres. Sena noticing my concern said that in the jungle we had to be prepared, so tools and pump were essential. He added that Rat was a fast rider if we needed to make a quick get-away. I noted the ominous 'quick get-away' to discuss later. Our first stop was to feed up our riders. I shifted around a bowl of fish noodles in grey liquor while everyone else slurped and noisily sucked out the 'best bits' from the bones before up-ending their dishes and tucking away the dregs with relish. That morning's noodles would have to keep me going for a bit longer I thought.

Rat was dispatched to market to get me a hat - I'd lost my own and the late morning sun was fierce. He returned with a child-size cap brightly embroidered with US Army. It offered very little protection and I imagined the rather interesting suntan mark that it would produce, perched on my baldhead by the end of the day. Leaving town we stopped to get petrol and more air in Rat's back tyre. I seemed to be the only one worried that it needed pumping up already. But we were away - the last tarmac for days.

Rat spoke no English and I no Khmer beyond hello, thank you and good luck so it was going to be a pretty solitary ride. I looked at the brown paddies trying to imagine the intense green I had witnessed on my first visit to Cambodia. Then the roads were a mess of mud and in places a vehicle could sink to its waistline. Now anything on the move produced a choking cloud of dust.

Palms punctuated the flat landscape into the distance like ink splodges on a sky of dirty blue blotting paper. I was idly making up pictures and wondering what a psychiatrist might make of my compositions when the bike hit a pothole. My feet shot off the foot rests and the shock that hit my arse whipped up my spine and flicked my head so far back that my mouth opened like a moneybox. I flailed around and found the grab bar which stopped me from tumbling off the back but in doing so I also found the many nasty repairs that had been made to the frame - the sharp and untidy welds took the skin off my knuckles. I was still fussing to find a good hold when another hole whipped my

neck. Instinctively avoiding the sharp frame I managed to grab Rat somewhere under his armpits as my legs swung forward. Somehow I got back into shape but still seeing stars I looked up to see Sena calmly bobbing along in front, one hand free smoking a cigarette.

Thankfully after an hour or so we stopped in a pleasant village for a refreshing drink of sugar cane juice. Here I exchanged my hat for something more suitable at a roadside stall and dug out my facemask. Sena handed around some ciggies and chatted with the locals and Rat went off to find a puncture repair. A couple of kids were doing all the work at the tyre shop while family life went on around them. I tried to keep thoughts of health and safety out of my mind as a toddler in a baby walker scooted through the assorted tools and implements on the dirt floor. A boy of about 7 was doing our job. He had such an air of authority that even the boy nearly twice his age was content to assist; passing tyre leavers and helping him crank up the old compressor. A rudimentary press made from an old piston filled with burning diesel heat sealed an old bit of inner tube over the hole but it seemed far from certain that the leak had been fixed. Judging by the number of patches already dotted round the tube it had seen better days but with optimism and air in the tyre we swung back onto the red road.

Though there was no tarmac involved some highway improvements were underway up the road. Sharp lumps of rock defined the traffic lane as we entered the great hall of dust. Workers with flags made valiant attempts to regulate the up and down flow. Everyone ignored them and we slalomed the rocks and the oncoming traffic in a pea-souper. In between ducking out of the onslaught of grit and vehicles, images were presented to me as if in a dream sequence; a child on a bicycle far too large for it wobbled out of the gloom, a little pony with pompom and bells hauling a family jingled by and beside the road two little dots probably no more than three or four walked hand in hand.

Further North agriculture gave over to forest and a high wall of trees and thick undergrowth bordered the route; the road became an orange stripe in the green. This was it I thought, proper jungle, and cheered my good fortune to be out here doing it for real. We were off the main route now it seemed as there was hardly any traffic to kick up the dust and whilst I still had to concentrate on the road, scanning ahead for holes, the travelling became easier. The temperature had dropped a couple of notches and the air was noticeably fresher. I imagined that we were on the edge of a forest that could stretch up to the border with Laos, getting lusher and thicker by the mile. I wanted to look up to watch the blur of green against the blue, to stretch out my hands to catch the moisture in a perfect 'Sound of Music, Von Trap Family running over the brow of the hill' moment. It was a short-lived pleasure as a pall of thick smoke up ahead grabbed it back like a spoilt child.

As Sena and Ret entered the plume it swirled and closed behind them. For a moment they were lost but we found them stopped beside an area a few acres wide that had been flattened and was ablaze, the trunks of the smaller trees looked like they'd been crudely hacked while the more sizeable ones had been sawn.

There was no one around to fight the flames and I asked Sena "what's happening here?" He just shrugged and said, "it's fuckin stupid". He pulled a hand held GPS device out of his bag and took a position and snapped a few photos. This was nothing new to him it was obvious but I tried to get my head round why someone would hack down the forest and set light to it. Just torch it and leave it to burn. Everything was tinder dry and every few minutes a sheet of flames shot up the trees that edged the clearing. "Why do they burn it?" I asked hoping for some

logic. "Because they have something to burn." Grim faced he got back on his bike and we rode off. With depressing regularity we passed more areas of smouldering jungle and without stopping Sena logged a GPS waypoint and snapped a shot with his digital camera, talking into a small Dictaphone as we went. It would be a catalogue of destruction.

The road was breaking up again but if there was any consolation to be taken from the worsening road at least its harshness postponed any real realisation of what I was witnessing. Now though the bumps had a sharper edge to them and the backend squirmed from side to side. I knew why we'd stopped. The tyre was flat again. Sena and Ret realising that we weren't behind turned back. A small bickering broke out between Rat and Sena. Sena kicked the tyre, seeming to make out that Rat was exaggerating, and gestured that he should just get on with it. I wondered why he didn't just use the pump to get us to the next tyre repair but decided to stay out of it. Then it became clear that I had become part of the conversation and obvious references were being made to my weight. I took umbrage to this and joined the fray adding very little but making the point that I was no way the heaviest. Sena gave me a stern 'stay out of this look' so I waited for the conclusion. Which was a Khmer, "if you think it's frickin rideable help yourself!" With that Sena picked up the gauntlet and bombed off alone on our bike. Rat sent him a few quiet curses and the three of us set off after him. What a revelation. Even three up and squeezed in the middle, Ret's machine was comfortable. Whilst Rat's bike had virtually no suspension at all, this bike had springs that worked; they soaked up every jolt that in California would have made me a fortune in whiplash claims. Envy is a terrible thing.

Despite the flat tyre Sena was making amazing time, probably driven on by bloody mindedness; he'd disappeared but I was enjoying the sprung ride. Quite expecting to find him in a heap, instead we found him at a roadside stall some twenty minutes later. The tyre was already off and an old stick of a man had the repair underway. Clearly smug with making it this far and well ahead of us he sat drinking a lurid coloured drink. As we went to join him a little guy rushed at me giving me a start. About six inches from my face he stopped and grinned a toothless grin and then raised a stump of an arm blown off to the elbow in a quick salute, "OK?" He kept on enquiring OK, OK? and saluting in quick succession looking like a flightless chick till I said, " yes, OK!" and he giggled and scuttled off. I decided to join the boys in one of the lurid drinks, a concoction of crushed ice, tinned milk and pink and lime fluorescent flavourings topped with a glace cherry. They wanted to know whether I liked it, I said, "we have these all the time at home, they're called the Preah Veah Sunset." My weak joke got a big laugh, its one of the advantages of travel.

There'd been a lot of clearance here but a little way up the road one tree towered out of the scrub. "See that?" said Sena. That's 'The Hiding Tree'. It's a Spirit Tree." He went on to tell me the legend how once some people found this tree in the forest and decided to come back with saws to cut it down. It was huge and would make them all rich. When they returned it was gone. The next day when they came to look again it was back. This time they had their saws with them and set to work but the tree was so hard it broke the sharp teeth of the saw without leaving a mark on the bark. Fearing that it had a spirit they left it alone. Here it stands protected by the spirit though from time to time it's said to disappear. I walked up to take a look. It was indeed a magnificent tree; probably four peoples combined arm lengths in circumference. It had been adorned with an orange sash in the Buddhist fashion and a small concrete 'spirit house' had been built at its base. I gave the trunk a hug to the amusement of passers by. Anything of size close by had been cut down leaving a low dense mess of growth. It was a sad reminder of what was there before and somehow like finding a thatched cottage on a rough 70's council estate. Maybe the melancholy blocked any connection but I asked it to watch over what was left there.

The repair was done and the actual Preah Vear sunset was nearly upon us. I didn't fancy being on this road in the dark and I hoped we weren't far from our stop for the night. In the dusk light we came across a string of new settlements, poorly made huts by the road. There were big patches of cleared forest, scraped back to the dust and the remains burned in a hundred pyres. It looked more like vandalism than agriculture. I couldn't understand why poor people would just burn valuable wood. It didn't make sense. Somebody was trying to do something about it as there were signs along the roadside, which read, 'Please don't cut me anymore' and 'Kill the forest, kill yourself' but the settlers seemed intent on doing both.

As darkness fell we got another puncture. I was knackered and just sat crushed in the road as another argument ensued. We switched bikes again but this time Sena took Ret with him. At least I was back on the comfy bike but I really had had enough. After the augment Rat was living up to his name and was not happy about being on a strange bike in the dark; he missed a gear and fumbled for the head beam switch. Sena was obviously caning it ahead and Rat was going for it too, I was beginning to get scared. Then in my peripheral vision I saw something run out and then there was a bump and a yelp, it was puppy. It was in the road squealing and squealing. Rat wasn't going to stop and in the moments I hesitated to shout stop, it became too late. I was miserable. I hope we'd just winged it or maybe someone would end its suffering but I couldn't get the sound out of my head.

Just on the edge of town we caught up with Sena and Ret, they'd given up on it. Sena commandeered the good bike and we left the riders to push the crippled one for the last kilometre or so.

7 No-good Guys

The Provincial capital boasted rooms with bathroom-attached and I was more than happy to shell a few extra dollars for the luxury. An en-suite jet wash would have been the go though. As I sprayed off my 'dust on tan' the shower splattered with red in a remake of 'Psycho'. I couldn't help but do a dark Anthony Perkins, "Mother, mother! Blood, blood!" I played with my gruesome reflection in the mirror and cheered up.

Feeling surprisingly chipper I met Sena and the riders and we headed off for something to eat. Tbeng Meanchay, or 'TBY' as its known is not big on nightlife, a few TV, stroke Karaoke bars looked busy and had strings of motos lined up like horses outside the saloon but otherwise the main street was dark. A little way from the centre there was a restaurant with a proper menu, which obviously catered for the NGO market. Tonight there were no westerners there except me. A big table of Forest Rangers in uniform looked to be having a bit of a night out and a guy in a supermarket style security outfit sat at a corner table. We ordered up some beer and I anticipated with relish the first glass going down in one. I was beginning to feel a little peaky below the belt but I reckoned the best way to deal with a doubtful belly was to feed it up. The boys plumped for a Cambodian style fondue, cook your own arrangement; a domed hotplate with a large lump of pork fat to melt into a reservoir for basting and plates of raw meat to griddle on top. Down wind I began to smell like a bacon butty stall but the copious flow of beer with ice took my mind off it.

A hard glint from the security guards belt declared that he wasn't exactly toy town after all and that in his big shiny holster he had an equally shiny gun of the 'make my day' variety. Sena nodded and smiled at him and then guessing he didn't speak English told me that he was the businessman's bodyguard. The said businessman was addressing the Forest Rangers who'd gone quiet since he rose to speak. Sena said, "You should hear what he's saying." With his back to the ranger's table Sena quietly interpreted. The businessman had opened with, "I need to know that you are all with me?" And to reinforce his point, "If you are not you should know that I can sell your jobs." There was menace in what he was saying yet it was at odds with the reaction of the Rangers who seemed to receive the words with nodding agreement. It was total acceptance of complete corruption. I was stunned. He went on, and clearly this was subtext to a scam they understood, "you don't need to worry about the police or the military; I'll take care of them. If you want to cut a tree then you must say that it is from the Community Forest or it is needed for a school or such." I said to Sena, "surely these guys are the protectors of the forest?" He gave me a look of 'you have much to learn'. This is how it was. There weren't any good guys to look after the forest; they were all in it together the rangers acting as the businessman's security guards, protecting his share in the robbery. As the businessman concluded his speech he encouraged each Ranger to make an oath to all present that he was looking out for his brother Ranger. I couldn't believe what I was witnessing. One after another they solemnly pledged to all assembled some kind of allegiance. As if there was something honourable in their endeavour. It was as corrupt as a paedophile addressing a party of conspiring churchmen.

The main business over they filed out past our table to take a piss in the bushes, chattering like teenagers let down from the coach on a daytrip. I was alone, the only one in the house shocked by what was going on; this was my baptism, an introduction to the way it was. There was nothing secretive about it everything was completely open. The rangers had sold out; the forest heroes had gone bad. I'd been cut with a sharp blade and the sting was just beginning to set in. Thankfully before the full implications of what I'd seen dropped on me Sena chinked my glass with a smile. He'd seen a Westerner's shock at this kind of blatant corruption before I was sure because he said "It will be part of my report. That's all we can do now." I realised that there was at least some good guys like him on the case. I wanted to understand how this was happening. He said he'd explain the situation to me but now was probably not a good time for obvious reasons. I decided to try and shut the shits on the other table out. Though my brain was tumbling there was nothing else to do.

In need of a distraction I quizzed Sena on his Pol Pot years. Meeting any Khmer over the age of twenty-five I wonder how they survived those horrible times. What struck me about this guy was how well his personality had adapted for survival. He's quiet and secretive yet can be big, friendly and charming. He gives very little away yet uses his exuberant friendliness very effectively. Sena is forty-two so I was intrigued to hear his story.

It's wonderful the way that simple English can strip away pretence. Ask somebody in the West what he or she does for a living and they will beat about the bush. Talked up or down it will all be couched in coded messages. Sena said simply, "I have high intelligence; in the army they realised this and I was ordered to give lessons to a Khmer Rouge (KR) General. Even though he was stupid I taught him well and I became his aid and read for him." Bearing in mind the KR killed anyone tainted with an education this was a high-risk strategy, I said. He dismissed the suggestion, "I have high intelligence", without a smidgen of arrogance. I told him about my experience in New Zealand with the big Kauri tree and how I wanted to find out more about our connections with the spirits in the forest. He told me that it was the discussion back in Phnom Penh about spirit trees that convinced him to bring me along. "When you hugged that tree today," he said, "I was thinking, Ken is a sweet man". Bless him, I thought.

The waitress continued to ply us with beers chilled with big lumps of ice and a warm fuzziness overtook me. The little tiffs of the day seemed to have been forgotten and Ret and Rat were happily picking the last from the plates. Sena was cheerfully telling me Khmer jokes that weren't funny, because he had to explain the punch lines, but I was grateful for his positivity in the face of so much to be unhappy about. The place had cleared and the booze was beginning to remind my body that I'd been up since 'you must be joking o'clock'. Sena's simple English had become more complicated as my eyes became weights. The power went off and as the candles were lit I was granted an excuse for my bed.

8 Alien Rumble

As my head hit the pillow I wondered what my spine would feel like in the morning, without the anaesthetic of half a dozen beers. There was no doubt about my gut though; I reckoned the Preah Veah cocktail had seen to that for sure.

I woke up in one of those disorientated states looking at a strange ceiling for a moment before rewinding to the point where I'd speculated on my physical state last night. I did a tentative audit. The spinal column though achy seemed OK, I tested for movement and everything appeared to work. Then a major personal plumbing event, together with a sharp stab of gripe, added urgency to the events. I was glad for bathroom attached.

Next door to our hotel was a big timber breakfast restaurant, which as Sena had granted us all a bit of a lay in was pretty much finished for the day at eight o'clock. Sena turned on the charm and they cooked us up a nice fresh starter for the day with lashings of coffee with slugs of sweet tinned milk. This was my first sight of PBY in daylight, there wasn't really much to see. Just a wide strip heading north and south, a scruffy attempt of a monument in the centre, a scattering of commerce and an intermittent traffic of Land Cruisers and motos that kicked up a bit of dust. Rat had a new tyre fitted while we had breakfast and we looked better set for a puncture-free day. With water and a few provisions packed for the road we were off. Sturdy red timber buildings lined the first kilometre out and then it was cleared agriculture and then open forest. The first bumps of the day thankfully didn't feel as bad as I imagined they might though the gripe in my belly was ominous.

We were on our way to an ancient hilltop Temple about one hundred kilometres from PBY. A route up close to the borders with Laos and Thailand and then West to Prasat Preah Vihar, an Angkorian monument built as part of the Angkor Wat complex. We would have to make a bit of a dent in the route back south to Siem Reap by nightfall too. It was going to be a long day.

The forest here reminded me of the open woodland typical of a London park. It was pleasant without being stunning. This whole area was Khmer stronghold during the later part of the conflict that ended in the early nineties. It's one of the most heavily mined regions in the country and there are red skull and cross bone warnings dotted all along the roadside bordering the forest. I hoped that I wasn't going to get caught short as it would be too dangerous to go into the bushes. Squatting in the road though wasn't something I quite had my head round.

We passed a few Buddhist monks carrying banners and flags which seemed particularly bizarre as there was no-one for miles, but then I realised that these were stragglers behind a column of a hundred or so marching monks. Their orange robes, fluttering flags and banners against the red road made for quite a spectacle. A blue duotone flyer announced a countrywide march for peace and the environment. A number of marchers not in robes were wearing t-shirts,

which depicted monks showing villagers how to replant the forest. There was such sincerity about their actions. A little way up the road distorted and over amplified music from a pagoda called the procession.

As if conceived by Roald Dahl this was the road of the unexpected. I looked up trying to make out the oncoming vehicle. I had a mental game with myself of 'don't tell me' trying to recognise it before it became obvious. But even upon us it was difficult to believe that it was a tractor hauling a Dragon Boat a good forty-foot long. Then there was another one and I fumbled to get my camera out but it was too late. I kicked myself for missing the shot. Then the god of the holiday slide granted me another go. Now unmistakable two more dragon boats approached. I was ready but my camera was set to review mode, agh! I quickly turned to shoot mode and grabbed one reasonable pic. The single guard atop the last boat gave me a menacing look and ducked down out the way as Sena snapped a final shot. We all looked at each other in amazement clearly this wasn't an everyday thing. It was obviously a new business opportunity.

The road surface here was ideal for heavy vehicles and was probably created by the logging industry. It was hard and wide but it had a small ripple produced by a large tracked vehicle pushing a dozing blade. It's probably hardly noticeable in a luxury land cruiser or a truck but on a moto without suspension it was an uncomfortable and harsh continuous vibration. On UK motorways it's a device used to ensure sleepy drivers don't stray onto the shoulder of the road; a Rumble Strip. Since we left PBY I'd had gripe but this incessant agitation was beginning to replicate something that NASA might have subjected potential astronauts to in the early days. Injected with a pathogen and vibrated to a blur. Now there was an Alien in my gut trying to punch its way out, it felt like I was going to explode.

It had been a long time since anything unusual happened and I'd become focused on developing a riding position that would protect my spine. I found by creating a triangle of my upper body and resting heavily on my knees I could absorb more of the shock through my arms. I started to grade the rumble strip from one to ten. Grade one is a mild vibro and I imagined grade ten would be enough to have us off. Though it was mostly grade four on the scale we'd had a few good grade seven's already. Violent enough to throw my feet off the pedals and vibrate me down the saddle till Rat and I looked like a multi-limbed Indian god in an electric chair. As the road narrowed the rumble strip gave way to deep sand. Up to a foot deep or more in places and we squirmed our way along. It was very slow going, never more than second gear at best. Rat had to use his feet to keep us up much of the time; it was the kind of riding that wears you out quickly. This was a route that seemed to have been overlooked by the loggers, maybe the heavy concentration of landmines kept them out of the forest.

We stopped for a break at what must have been a workers shelter. Sena explained that the forest here was made up from mainly resin trees. The production was a sticky solid resin. I picked off a souvenir; it had the heavy aroma of temple incense. Like all smells it invoked its own set of memories and triggered my neurons all the way back to a field in Sussex blending incense with a bunch of hippies in a blender. Cool fresh Sussex grass would have been refreshing now. We stretched out in the shade, the rest was welcome and we drifted off for a little while. The alien stirred me though and I slipped out in the hope of finding a discrete spot, Sena said from his doze "don't leave the path, there are mines here." There was to be no privacy or dignity for me. I imagined that this is how I'll feel the first day nurse takes my bedpan at the old peoples home. "Well-done Mr Finn!" "Thanks Matron."

Back on the road the sand reverted to rumble strip as we came to a major highway. I hated myself for cheering the prospect of what looked like a grade one logging road. It was a behemoth strip of straight hard red dirt. We turned west and bombed off. The little motor hummed like I'd not heard it before and my hat flipped like a kite on its strap round my neck.

9 Temple Subterfuge

It was already lunchtime as we arrived in Choam Ksant but we planned to keep going, this was a quick stop to get petrol and a drink from our bottles. We were ready to press on when Sena gestured with a small movement of his hand that we should sit for a while. I sensed that he might have found what ever it was he was looking for so we sat in the shade of a storefront and watched. He was clearly at work as the volume on the big smiles and belly laugh cranked up. The bonhomie brought in a few more curious people to the little throng he had generated. Like a clever angler he'd put out the bait and now danced the worm, earnestly nodding as individuals offered up information; pointing the way that something or someone had come and then pointing in the direction it had gone. He let the line slack whilst the shoal offered up its choicest morsels before he selected the best specimens keeping them back for a quiet word as he let the others go. It became clear that we weren't going anywhere for a while.

I joined Rat in a dish of cashew fruits. A bizarre looking fruit that wears its nut on the outside like a coat hook. It bruises easily which is probably why we don't get to see them in England. The juicy flesh is like a stringy plum tomato with a flavour and colouring of a sharp apple. It's eaten dipped in a mix of sugar and chilli. It's a refreshing treat that's very more-ish. The mobile butcher pulled up looking like an extra from a Nam movie, his old fatigues splattered with blood. The bush telegraph was working, as he was here to add his two-penny worth to what ever Sena had kicked up. A large sack that was wedged onto the frame of his moto dripped blood onto the hot exhaust. The congealed and partially cooked remains of recent cuts turned my stomach. He had that cheeriness that butchers have. It always scared me as a child.

Rat attempted a little conversation, it became more of a mime show after we'd exhausted our combined vocabulary of half a dozen words but it was fun. We mimed about the rumble strip and my flying head butts to his skull, the dust and the noises I made when the wind was knocked out of my lungs by a large bump. It was good to see him smile and to make a connection with him. He didn't laugh or smile easily and because of his sharp Chinese features he looked stern till his face cracked. I could see why Sena had chosen them both, they're good guys. Even the tiffs about the punctures the previous day had been more down to Sena being a bit of a Prima Dona.

Sena was winding up and now the conversation centred on me. They pointed to my shaved head and my orange shoulder bag. He said, "I've told them you're a monk and that I'm taking you to see the temple", I smiled and nodded going along with it but I decided it was definitely time for our little chat about what he was up to. The butcher hauled the carcass out of the sack and slammed it on the board mounted to his bike. With his big knife drawn he looked even scarier. Clearly this cut was for Sena as they did the universal butcher's 'little bit more, little bit less' routine. I asked, "Sena, why are you buying meat for goodness sake!?" "I've told them that I have relatives close by and we are going to visit. They would be less likely to talk to me if they thought I was an outsider. The meat will go off quickly so they'll believe that I really must be local."

A little way up the road we stopped outside a brand new concrete building set back from the road. Sena said, "Ken I need a picture of you in front of that building." It was clear from the distance he was shooting I would be a speck in the panorama. It was time for a few answers I thought. "Sena, what is this building and why do you need a photo?" He grinned, "This' why we're here," he said. Maybe I was being dim but I didn't get any connection. "OK, I'll explain. Did you hear about the shoot out over an illegal log convoy last week? It was in all the papers in Phnom Penh." I'd seen something but it was another headline in the routine content of shootings and murder. "Well I'm here to investigate. With what we already knew and what I just found out the story is that the Governor of Phnom Penh came up here with much political hype to deliver equipment to the new hospital that's behind you. The Japanese donated it but he made it his 'mission of mercy' to transport it up in trucks that he'd supplied.

Well he figured that these vehicles would be going back to Phnom Penh empty. It would be far better to fill them up with timber he had cut up here. We knew that much already, what we couldn't understand was why the Forest Rangers tried to do their job for once! Well it seems the Governor decided he wasn't going to pay the customary bribes and they tried to stop him. At the border with Kompon Thom the rangers set up a roadblock to extract their cash. The Governor's men had more guns and fired a few shots as a warning then shot out the tyres of the Ranger's vehicles and sped off to Phnom Penh where the trucks disappeared." As he got back on his bike he said with another grin, "Oh by the way, I told them back there that you might be interested in buying a Dragon Boat for your Pagoda in Thailand!" "Cheers! Use me and abuse me, why don't you?" I said with sarcastic humour. "So anyway, do you want to go to the Temple?" Sena called out as Ret started his bike. Although this was as far as Sena needed to go for the investigation it seemed foolish to come all this way and not see it. The temple was only twenty kilometres or so up the road. "Why not?" I shouted and we were off.

As we buzzed along the grade one strip the conversation replayed in my mind. I wondered if this was dangerous, and whether it was worth the spinal injury and the alien growing in my gut. It was undeniably the adventure I was looking for and I wondered how many drinks was this story worth back home? Sena was clever enough to keep us out of trouble I reckoned and I enjoyed the prospect of messing with the businessmens' corrupt system too.

The Prasat Preah Vihar Temple looks down from the cliff face of Chour Phnom Dangkrek Mountain onto lowland Cambodia from its perch five hundred and fifty metres above. It was built by a succession of monarchs beginning with Yasovarman I A.D.890 and ending with Suryavarman II the creator of Angkor Wat in A.D.1150. It's an important part of the Khmer history and more recently the scene of intense fighting. This was the last stand for the Khmer Rouge and their final surrender. The small village, at the base of the mountain serves as a stop for tourists wanting transport up to the temple and is also base for the NGOs working to clear the area of munitions. Signage proclaimed their projects and a big board beside the road displayed the objects to avoid if you want to stay alive. Not surprisingly there were no tourists awaiting transport. Dramatic as the location is, if you wanted to see splendid Angkorian Temples you'd go to Angkor Wat. That is unless you're a hardcore temple freak. But here I was, so close to the border that my phone welcomed me to Thailand.

After what we'd just ridden over it was hard to believe but the guys said that they wouldn't be riding up the mountain. Instead we negotiated a 4x4 vehicle to take us up for twenty US dollars, entry included. It was a jacked up old Nissan pickup that looked like a 'Big Foot' reject. As we started the serious climb on the very doubtful track the small kid that was riding on the doorsill jumped down to engage the four-wheel drive at the hub. He chucked down a large choc to stop us from flying down backwards and then manually engaged the drive. The driver told Sena that a moto had gone over the side last week and they had only just found the body because of the smell. It was just too dangerous to go looking because of the mines. About half way up we stopped as the steam coming from under the bonnet clearly meant it had over heated. There was some road building going on so we watched the bulldozer doing its stuff, carving out a new ledge from the side of the mountain for a while before the driver considered that it was cool enough to proceed. At the top a small community of mine clearance workers and their families live and work. They looked equipped with the latest detectors in flash banjo-shaped cases carried over their shoulders. As we got out of the pick-up a deep boom went off in the distance and I presumed it was a safe detonation.

The temple is built on a series of levels and arriving from this side of the mountain we were approximately midway up. The classic Angkorian style steps with the mythological serpent, the Naga as its handrail went down to the entrance, which the Thais have built a pristine road right up to. I'd have been gutted if I had come here just for the temple to find tourists in equally pristine trainers bussed in aircon from Thailand to the door. As it was there were few here and certainly no westerners. I hadn't seen one since we left Phnom Penh.

We walked up to the next tier. A string of souvenir sellers woke up as we approached but there was nothing I wanted. The familiar winey "Misstaar" call went out as we passed. It's something you get used to quickly at Angkor Wat. Then I saw an animal skin and went over to look; the vendor was asleep so I photographed everything on his stall, two Clouded Leopard skins, Antelope skins and horns, a Bear's paw and various other gruesome wildlife parts. One of the other stallholders shouted for him to wake up but I already had the evidence. Sena said, "They called you a bastard. They think you'll get them shut down." "Too bloody right I will!" We went up to the top and looked at the dramatic view back across Cambodia, it was indeed stunning but I was shagged out and angry. Sena said that it would be dark by the time we reached our stop for the night so we should get going. "Best not to let the guy on the stall get to you, we'll do something about it when we get back to Phnom Penh. I know the people to talk to, OK?" "OK" I said.

10 Back To Chucks

Wearing my sunglasses for protection against the grit I had a preview of the road in the failing light. Thankfully as we left the temple the rumble strip was on medium setting as I was hurting, tired and the Alien was getting angry. The quickening dark was on us but the two riders used their combined lights to shine the way. Buzzing along side by side the potholes were better discernable though I was more worried about encountering something like the beaten up wooden bridges we'd crossed today. Ret and Rat seemed confident enough so I tried to stay focused on keeping my back straight and chin tucked in to avoid another painful whiplash.

As the air cooled down, settlers had taken to their plots and the burning resumed in earnest. We came to what could have been taken for a plane crash. The scene was something I'd viewed on TV in another context; a long wide strip of flattened forest with multiple fires and debris hanging from the trees, toiling faces lit by the flames. It was a disturbing carnage and I wondered how long the forest could sustain this daily onslaught. The urgency caught my breath.

On the dark road the dust added another veil to unlit figures, bicycles and vehicles that dived out from nowhere. Dogs had a death wish. The riders seemed to have developed their night sight, weaving and ducking the apparitions, occasionally stabbing at the brakes. We stormed through another surreal dream as our lights sent rays into a fog of powdered earth. The settlements were behind us and the jungle once again defined the road. Rat and Sena had dropped behind us in single file as the road surface broke up making side-by-side riding impossible.

Up ahead, trees had been used to block the road and a figure stood in a guarding posture. Rat was not preparing to stop. I didn't like the look of it and I thought it would be better not to be recognised as a westerner. Pulling up my facemask I reckoned I was dusty and scruffy enough to pass for a Khmer in the dark.

I braced myself but in an impressive slalom action we weaved through the barricade as the guard made a lunge for us. We stopped about a hundred yards up the road to see that Ret and Sena had been caught. Rat said something to me in Khmer, he sounded worried and I hoped it was not about to go bad. Stories of night time kidnappings flashed through my mind. After what seemed a long time the guard's body language appeared less threatening and I began to trust Sena's ability to talk his way out of a dodgy situation. I breathed a sigh as the bobbing of the headlight signalled they were through and Rat and I moved off. It was a bit of a reality check. What was a suburban chap like me doing out in the jungle at night?

All I wanted as we arrived in the village of Xang Cung Thmay was to lie down, anywhere would do, and I just wanted it now. It was getting late for these parts and only a few oil lamps were alight on the road. We pulled up at a couple of houses; Sena appeared to be begging for somewhere to stay. Then improbably we pulled into a little guesthouse. The rooms had been furnished in the boudoir brothel style, red synthetic satin sheets and plush cushions but dual purpose or not they looked inviting. Sena said, "shower and be ready in half an hour, we're going to my friends for dinner." I just wanted to collapse and thought maybe I'd make my excuses and crash. I decided to see what I felt like after a hose down. The electricity was short lived and was obviously provided just for room sales purposes. Without the fan the temperature in the room rocketed and the prospect of a cold beer drove me out.

We went back to one of the houses we'd stopped at earlier. A face appeared at a gap and recognising us a few more planks were unhitched from a frame in the front of the property to let us in with our bikes. There was a warm glow from the lamps and candles dotted around and a delicious aroma wafted from the kitchen. I was introduced to Chuck and his family; they were strikingly beautiful – high cheek boned and sparkling eyes. They were cooking for us and had got a case of beer in too. It was a lovely welcome. Small mats were laid out on a low table come bed come bench, the kind to be found in most Cambodian homes. They're ideal for hanging out with friends or family. You can set out dinner and eat cross legged then clear away and add a few cushions and you have a couch. It's a functional solution for a dirt floor. Being of sturdy timber construction I was surprised to see a Termite mound in Chucks main room. Sena told me that this was in fact considered good fortune as it indicated that good spirits were residing there. Having Termites as houseguests is also practical as the mound draws up moisture into the surrounding soil and the house is less dusty.

Chuck and the family fussed around to make sure we were comfortable and I found the perfect position flat on my back on the table. A cushion was placed under my head. It was bliss. I was content to stay out of the conversation and let the beer dull the aches till dinner was served. It was full of love and kept coming till I couldn't sit cross-legged anymore. After everything was cleared away Chuck showed us their holiday snaps. The family in bright holiday clothes, a Vietnamese theme park in the background. It was a nice juxtaposition. My eyelids were slipping and I was struggling to keep up with Sena's English when he said to me, "its OK Ken, you can sleep now." The release was immediate. A couple of hours later they propped me on a bike for the short ride to my red boudoir.

11 Badlands

Despite a loving dinner the Alien was unappeased. It's time clock answered to an earlier measure and I had to follow suit so I'd been up for a while when Sena knocked. Trying to be as nonchalant as possible I said, "so Sena was that dangerous at the roadblock last night?" "Oh no, he was just trying to extort money. He cut a tree and it fell the wrong way into the road. He couldn't afford to hire a chainsaw to cut it up so decided to drag some more trees onto the road to make a barricade and then charge people to pass to raise enough for a saw." "He looked pretty serious to me", I said. "Don't worry", he said before going onto what he obviously came to say. "I have to tell you our code for today. The town we are going through really hate my organisation so don't mention it by name and don't talk about logging. OK? If you do want to ask me something then you must use 'rice' if you want to talk about logs and 'farmer' if you want to talk about loggers. Right?" "Right", I said. "Oh and can I get a picture of you with the owner of this place?" "Why not?" I said. It was becoming our little catch phrase. "He used to be a Khmer Rouge officer. I found out a bit more about him yesterday, now he's paymaster to the military in the illegal log business." I was happy to do my part, the monk lined up for a photo with the gangster – I smiled, he didn't and we were off. All being well we'd be in Siem Reap by early evening.

We dropped back at Chuck's to pick up some provisions for the road and I got the chance to say good-bye properly. We gave them some money for the food and beer, which, they quietly accepted. He appeared to have a thriving little business, a shop front lined up with car batteries that he re-charged with a generator connected up to an old cultivator. These were the villager's electricity supply.

Our route south took us through the fringes of the Kulen Prum Tep Wildlife Sanctuary. It's exactly the kind of jungle I hoped to see, tall thick and luxuriant – the type that has thirty-two shades of green. The road was wide, solid and ideal for loggers. This area is probably the origin of the wildlife parts I'd seen the previous day too. As we rounded a corner we disturbed two chainsaw drivers cutting up a giant of a tree. They had already made large incisions with their saws, the blades of maybe five foot or more designed for this kind of work. We stopped a little further out of sight for Sena to make notes and take a GPS waypoint. The saws had stopped now. Sena said that usually the lookouts would have warned them especially if there was a Barang (westerner) in the locality. Maybe we were all filthy enough to pass the watch without causing a stir.

On the outskirts of Anlong Veng the river that flows beside the town is red with erosion and lined with dead trees. It's a fitting entrance for the former home of the K.R. top table. All the Brothers from Pol Pot, Brother No.1 down, held up here for nearly a decade. The stronghold fell apart in 1998 as Pol Pot avoided justice by dying up by the Thai border before the last stand and surrender at Prasat Preah Vihear. Riding in it feels like entering a biker's bar dressed as a hippy.

We stopped for something to eat and a rest. The town had a bad vibe but I was grateful to get off the bike for a while, I was feeling pretty awful. We sat in a karaoke restaurant that was without charm. A Thai happy sing-along played and froze in quick succession on the TV screen. The DVD continued to skip but the waitress either didn't notice or didn't care as the entertainment stuttered its brain numbing torture through the P.A. The spirit house by the bar was littered with the pink toilet tissue that is dispensed at the table as a 'napkin on a roll' and the couple of offerings that had long ago dried up told the story. I looked at Sena and said "the kind spirits left here a long time ago." "They corrupted them," he said. It was all crashing in on me and he picked up on it. "Do you want me to get you a taxi for the rest of the way? You don't look happy." It was true I'd lost it. It was all flying about in my head, the burning of the forest and the wildlife trade – the corruption. I was at best the spy's assistant in a war where the odds were stacked against us. I wasn't going to give in though even if I did feel completely useless.

I said I was OK; I just needed a rest and a snack. I told him that I was grateful for the opportunity to do the trip, it had been a great experience and that I didn't intend to jump ship on the last day. He said, "you wait, the next trip we won't be on bikes. Next month I'm going right along the border with Vietnam and in Mondulkiri province you hire an Elephant to get around!" "Wow, that would be fantastic. What's going on there?" I said, lifting out of the gloom. "We want to check what's happening, to see if any of the cross border routes are being used by *'Farmers to take rice'* across. The main routes are quiet but there's bound to be something going on. Do you want to come with me?" "Why not?" I said and we laughed at our little in-joke.

As Sena tucked into his noodles I looked out on the town; I wanted to take everything in. The wonders of the forest had been exchanged for a few Western beads it seemed. A youth with a new motor scooter postured, feeding his ego. There was no display of joy at his new toy only the implied status of ownership. He'd learnt 'cool'. How easy it was to spot the ludicrous illusion that we're wedded to in the first world that possessions make the man. And what a crap deal, like his friend's new mobile phone conspicuously on view, these objects of desire were destined to be rubbish.

The waitress fussed over her split ends, her youth and near perfect form brought her no joy either. She was sullen and shuffled her feet on the dirt floor. Perhaps discontent that her good looks had not brought her anything more than a waitress job in a dump, in a dead end town.

We sat on remnants of the forest. The wooden restaurant furniture was huge and wasteful in its construction and had been carved and turned into the grotesque. Its deep varnish probably hadn't been cleaned since the day it was applied. Perhaps it was a spirit tree that we sat at, trashed to buy those new trinkets that were to bring no lasting pleasure. The Spirits had surely been corrupted as Sena suggested. There was no happiness here only the same discontent that can be seen anywhere, feelings of emptiness are fed with useless shiny 'stuff'. I wondered vaguely whether I was trying to fulfil something of my own with this adventure. It was time to move on and I was cheerful to be leaving but I sent the place some love, it needed plenty.

As we left town a white car buzzed us, it hung just in front till the dust made it impossible to see or breathe and we had to stop. Sena hollered his customary "fuckin Stupid!" Rat had got a mouthful of dust and coughed it up while adding his curse to the taxi driver. The road was getting busier now and we were accumulating a considerable layer of dirt.

At a big expanse of water the road ran along a man-made dyke for a mile or two and I wondered how many Khmer Rouge workers died in its construction. The water level was low and between the patches of weed mud flats had formed. Wading birds and man seemed to be in competition for whatever fish survived. We stopped and Sena went over to speak to a figure on the bank; he handed him a cigarette and squatted down. He was working. Just then the white car, its windows blacked out came flying back the other way. We stepped off the road as it billowed past us at high speed. It was making me paranoid. Up the road a big truck loaded with timber had broken down and a couple of guys were at work underneath. I was bored hanging around and thought I'd go take a look. Sena guessing where I was going gave me a very discrete 'don't go there' look. So I wandered back to the bikes. A couple of cigarettes later he shook the guy's hand and crossed back to rejoin us. He gave me a little satisfied grin that another small piece of information had just come his way, "now I have 150 percent". As we passed the truck I saw a pool of oil underneath, the driver and his mate still clanking with tools. Its load was the half round waste produced by squaring logs indicating that large trees were being processed nearby.

I settled in to keeping it together for the last big chunk of mileage. This was badlands and there was little in the way of inspiring landscape to take my mind off the rumble strip and the nagging concern that there was something sinister about the car with the black windows. The motor whirred on like white noise and I scanned the red road ahead in a deep hypnosis waiting for the next rut to whip my neck and test the integrity of my sphincter. Then paranoia changed places with monotony as maybe an hour later here it came again, the anonymous car kicking up the grit and forcing Rat to take his hand off the throttle to shield his eyes. Sena seeing it coming dug into his pocket for his camera; it seemed a tad foolhardy to me. The boot lid was flapping open but the black windows obscured any view of the occupants. For a moment Ret and Sena held alongside the vehicle before dropping back into the plume of red earth. We pulled up while Sena took a GPS reading. He grinned and waffled something more about percentages, sparked up a cigarette and we pressed on.

We had been making good progress and we swung into a roadside café for lunch. I had no appetite just a continual churning gripe. As the boy's lunch was served up the alien asked, where's mine with a pang of hunger? It did look good. A bowl of boiled eggs, fresh and aromatic herbs, bread and little bowls of mixed seasoning. I was about to change my mind when Sena said, "Westerners don't like these." I asked why. He said, "They have erm, babies inside. Babies, is that how you say it?" I thought for a minute and realised that he meant chicks. "Chicks?" I said. "Yes, chicks that's it. Yes sometimes they leave them too many days and they make a noise when you boil them." I winced. "Look here's the head", he said as he pulled out the little form. "Too much information Sena," I said as he chortled.

Outside a new land cruiser pulled up and a well-built guy got out. He was wearing immaculate fatigues and a crisp white T-shirt with a large calibre handgun tucked in his waistband. He had 'don't fuck with me' written all over him. He talked into a mobile phone and looked down the road in the direction we'd just come. "He's a Protector", said Sena without being obvious, "protector of the log trade. He's probably waiting for the lorry that broke down up the road." The guy continued to pace about then sure enough about fifteen minutes later the old truck stopped outside. The driver and the protector exchanged a few words and then they were both off. "Hey Ken, did you see what was in the boot of the white car?" "No, and that was a bit risky taking a pic wasn't it", I said. "It was full of timber, it was so full they couldn't shut the boot. I got a good shot of it" I was baffled, "what's the sense of running it about in a car", I said. "Well if I tell you that a cubic metre of really top grade timber is worth a thousand dollars at the Vietnam border, it makes a lot of sense!" I gave him a 'you're taking the piss!' look. "This is what we're up against here, a good job in Cambodia like a teacher pays thirty dollars a month." "I thought they were following us!" I said. "No they just like to scare you to make sure you stay out of their business." I wondered how everything got so skewed that a boot full of one tree could be worth so much and yet a forest of another could be so worthless that it was flattened and burnt. I asked him to explain. "I know it's fuckin stoopid!" He said acknowledging the contradiction before carrying on. "Well the stuff in the car was black wood, its very valuable but the trees that are left after the best are taken, well the businessman is not interested. The laws to stop the loggers say that if you take a saw to a tree you're processing it yet if you burn it, it is ok. The rangers will fine the poor farmer if they catch him with a saw." I pondered the crazy distortion. I'd seen how the rangers were in the pocket of the businessman so clearly they weren't going to bother him. He went on, "It is also illegal to transport logs so you see they have no choice." It was a recipe for pointless destruction. They couldn't cut the trees on their land to use them productively, sell them or move them. Legally all they could do was burn it. The laws to protect the forest had made the trees worthless. The rich avoided the law anyway and just got richer. In fact it seemed to me that the set up just ensured that the valuable trees became the property of the rich and the law ensured that the poor were kept away till it was time to reap the businessman's harvest. Mmm I wonder where we've seen that before I smiled to myself.

Back on the road the landscape was becoming more ordered. Well-established agriculture replaced the haphazard settlement of less than an hour ago. Then something I hadn't seen for three days jumped out from the side of the road; a traffic sign. It signalled a bend up ahead. As we turned the corner it felt as bizarre as entering a scene from The Wizard of OZ. The road surface became tarmac and a brightly painted moto rickshaw like something from Munchkin Land bobbed along with two fresh white tourists in the back. As we passed them they didn't even look at me, I was just another dusty Khmer. We had reached the northern most temples in the Angkor complex, Banteay Srei. It was tarmac all the way to Siem Reap.

12 Shark Soup

It was late in the afternoon when we arrived in Siem Reap but thankfully still ahead of schedule. Sena dropped me with a rickshaw rider at the corner of the main street and explained that it was his nephew. "He'll take you to a guest house and later he'll come and pick you up, we'll have a drink at my house, we can relax. Yes?" "Sure", I said, "I plan to get a massage if I can find 'The Seeing Hands' place." Rat and I shook hands and exchanged a smile; I didn't know whether I'd see him again. They rode off and I found myself back in tourist land.

Actually, tourist land isn't so bad if you're looking for creature comforts and by a lovely stroke of luck my guesthouse was next to 'Seeing Hands'. After a long wash down I deposited my road clothes, shoes and pack with the laundry girl and went next door. I visited Seeing Hands last time I was here and it became a regular treat. Finding an honest massage in S.E. Asia, one without extras is difficult and has put me off even trying in the past but here is different. Set up by a charity to help the blind find stable employment the operatives have all been trained in the art of massage. The name sums up the experience. It seems that they can see through their hands the knots that need working on. I had plenty. I groaned my way through the hour but emerged released and smiling. Maybe they have healing hands too.

My digestive system was completely shot though and I became resolved to wage a war of attrition on the Alien. I was going to starve the bastard. But first I needed one last meal. This was no time for a consideration of was it possibly a bit too spicy for a delicate tummy; this was war. The last supper was on the menu, Coconut curry and it was delicious. My appetite came back with a vengeance. I scoffed it down like a hungry dog and for a moment I felt the bliss and well-being found in the bottom of a can of Chum. It was short lived, my first salvo was met with a punch and a roar; the Alien was back to strength and ready for the fight.

Later Sena's nephew came to pick me up but explained there'd been a change of plan and we were to meet his uncle at the Shark Fin Soup restaurant. I was in no condition to eat anything more and I didn't know whether I would be able to restrain myself and upset my friends with a lecture on the evils of shark fin soup. I used the nephew's phone to call ahead. I started to explain but Sena interrupted, "I thought I'd buy you a Sea Food dinner, I know you can eat fish. We can have a few beers too" "Sena I can't eat Shark Fin soup", my statement met with silence, I could here him trying to get his head round; will eat fish but can't eat shark. Realising that this was going to be too complex an explanation to be done by phone I said, "I've already eaten, I'll just have a few beers OK?" "Sure, why not?"

The restaurant was a big tacky affair with a neon shark at the entrance. I was pleased to see Ret and Rat had come for dinner too. They were scrubbed up and looking dapper. Sena was in his best and introduced me to his other guest, a dashing looking man with a very eighties foppish haircut, which he flicked back to reveal a dazzling strip of white teeth. "He's a pilot," said Sena. "I used to fly Migs but they can't get the parts these days. Now I fly a balloon at Angkor Wat," said Jon, sounding like he'd learnt his English in the US. He was obviously a local hero and the waitresses hung on his shoulder; he flicked and grinned. I smiled at his contentment; there was a certain early John Travolta innocence about him. This association clicked the recognition switch I'd been looking for, seeing Sena with his hair brushed back in a quiff I realised he's an Asian Jaaames Brown! Whilst the boy's yakked in Khmer I amused myself with the idea of hanging out with the original Soul Brother and the Ultimate White Icon of Disco. I really admired the way that Sena could switch off from his work. I'd spent just three days on the road with him and already I'd seen enough to make me deeply sad and angry enough to rant about the destruction. Yet here he was honestly enjoying himself, the head of the table and a great source of laughter.

I flitted in and out of the banter over the evening but I was out more than in; the experiences of the last few days were sinking in but hearing the suggestion that Jon take me up for a flight in the morning had me back like a shot. The sunrise at Angkor is an unforgettable experience. The prospect of flying over it in a balloon had me all ears. Yep, weather permitting Jon said he'd take me up, just be there at five thirty. What a fantastic opportunity I thought.

Sena had moved on and was having a little fun with my monk identity with the others. Jon said, "This guy Sena is quite a spy, eh?" I laughed and agreed. He went on, "You know he's quite a hero too. He got jailed for his human rights work." A bit shocked, I looked at Sena, he grinned and said, "I haven't told you much about my life have I? Jon is talking about my work for Licadho, a human rights organisation. I got put in jail for supporting local people over the Sihanoukville toxic dumping." He asked me if I knew about it. It only got a mention in my guidebook and there was little detail; I wanted to know more. He went on to tell me how corrupt officials had allowed a shipload of toxic waste to be dumped on the outskirts of the port town. Three thousand tons of solidified waste laced with mercury from the Formosa Plastics Group of Taiwan, the world's largest manufacturer of PVC had been stacked out in the open in plastic sacks. The locals were told it was just building rubble. The poor people seeing that the sacks would be useful, ripped them from their contents. The plastic was used to make bags for going to the market and keeping fish, sleeping mats and even the 'rubble' had a value. It was later found all over town and even on one of the resort's beaches. No wonder they wanted to keep that last detail out of the guidebooks I thought. One of the Dockers who'd unloaded it quickly died and local people fell sick in their hundreds. As rats at the site started to die it came out that the waste was toxic and there was a mad panic. News of the death swept the town and rumours that it could even be nuclear triggered a frightening exodus in which four people died. As thousands fled the poor had nowhere to go. "They came to the Licadho offices; they were angry and ready to riot. We tried to help them use the law to deal with the situation. We wanted to calm them but the protests got violent. I wasn't even on the march but they still arrested me." He explained how he and another Licadho campaigner were made scapegoats. "They used pictures of us talking to the protesters who came to the office as evidence that we had incited the riot. It was fuckin stupid." Together with his co-worker they were jailed awaiting trial for three months before International pressure brought about their release. There were sham hearings but the focus was on the damage and looting done in the riot rather than the outrage of dumping toxic waste on land used by the community. "A Japanese campaigner from 'Human Rights Watch' wrote about us; it helped in getting our release but these days I have to use a different name." Sena shifted his attention back to the table. "And so! You guys, if you're going up in the balloon in the morning we better all finish here." Sena wanted to change the subject. It was probably the most I'd got out of him about the way things were but clearly there was more to his story. "Sena, that's all mad. Did they put the people responsible in jail instead? Your family must have been worried sick!" "We'll talk tomorrow, its late now." He was right four forty-five wasn't that far away but he'd done it to me again. He gave me one of his grins and I saw that we were building a friendship that would have time for talk; it was ok. We raised our glasses and cheered each other with the last of the beer.

I said goodbye to Ret and Rat, I asked Sena to tell them how great they'd been. It would take me a long time to get the sight of the back of Rat's head out of mine I said. They laughed. My praise seemed thin; I hoped it came through in the warmth of my handshake though. Quietly Sena and I agreed a decent bonus on their daily rate. I felt better for that. It was the end of an amazing trip but I had one more treat set for the morning and I was excited as a kid on Christmas Eve. I'd be awake at a quarter-to-five for sure.

13 Angkor Sunrise

I knew what Santa was bringing but couldn't wait to rip off the paper and sat grinning on the back of a moto on my way to a beautiful sunrise. The warm pre-dawn breeze rushed at my face and the giants of the forest towered up, their benevolent forms just visible against the dark blue sky. A small convoy of motos and moto drawn rickshaws were on their way to meet the glow starting to appear in the East. Anticipation was thick in the air as the gig was about to kick off. The star; the sun was on its way. We peeled off in the direction of the balloon visible in the west, orange as a Jaffa and swaying on a tether. Tether? Sounding in my head like an ungrateful kid who just got last years model when everybody on the street would be bound to be getting the latest. I wanted to have a little stamp at the prospect of a Tether. I had imagined serenely drifting over the temple, the chants of monks and the beeping of frogs the only thing audible above the breeze; the first to witness the breaking corona of the sun over the spires of Angkor Wat.

Instead the balloon was tied to the ground by a steel cable and winched up and down as a static viewing platform. Jon waved, flicked and grinned. He said, "I'm not sure whether we can go up, the wind is close to the maximum permitted. I will go up to check first." It's just a sissy breeze I said to myself in my adolescent strop. It was rapidly getting lighter and I was in a quandary. Should I just split and try to be among the crowds at Angkor Wat for the first rays or wait to see if it was going to happen. An over amplified racket had just started playing from close by and the generator that run the winch was humming away. What had happened to my perfect sunrise?

As Jon returned he said, "its seventeen knots and rising, the limits twenty two, but we'll go up." Below the gas-filled balloon there's a circular aluminium cage with none of the organic feel of a hot-air balloon. Jon, showed me the controls and dials. There's nothing to control though really, just up and down and some trim. He closed the gate on the cage and up we went. The sun had broken the horizon but low cloud prevented a view of the golden orb. Then at the cables limit the balloon gently swayed on the stiff breeze and Angkor did it's magic on me. Even the distorted music below became atmospheric. "Look, it's a wedding. That's where the noise is coming from" said Jon, pointing to a decorated building a quarter of a mile away. For him it was another day but he was still high on it. Last night I had imagined that he was ego driven and yet here was a fast jet pilot happily working the lever on an elevator. I felt at once both happy and ashamed of myself for my selfishness, my desire for the perfect experience. Which, after all was remarkable. The sun was up now and visible as a milky disk casting long misty shadows on the morning and bathing Angkor Wat in a soft lens light as it might have done a thousand years ago. It was a hawk's eye view of a splendid homage to god.

We stood quietly for ten minutes taking it in then Jon started our descent.

My moto boy said, "Breakfast?" Not yet I thought, "The Bayon next." I said. The Bayon temple is a pile of stones till you get close then huge carved faces emerge. The crowds were still at Angkor Wat a couple of miles away and I shared the cool meditative smiles of the Bayon with just a handful of people. The sun hadn't yet made its way down all the faces as I arrived and the shadows threw the carvings into deep relief. Inside the temple are a number of shrines and in the centre most sanctuary The Buddha is adorned with orange sashes and lavish materials that glitter in the multitude of candles lit around him. The statue is attended by the cutest of old ladies and she invited me to take Puja. We knelt together and she gave me a bunch of lighted incense to hold between my hands in prayer and to bow three times to Buddha. "Sok Sab Bay, Sok Sab Bay, Sok Sab Bay" Good Fortune and long life, she said with every dip in her gorgeous croaky Khmer. The yellow light from the candles and gold reflected on her crinkly face imparting a cherub like glow to her aged smile. She was as happy as a toffee and I imagined how cheerful I'd be having her in a corner of my house. Lucky Buddha.

Back outside I sat for a while on the cool stone watching the colour come into the many cheeks of the Jayavarman VII, the builder of The Bayon; as the sun warmed the last visages that look to all corners of the once vast Khmer empire.

My fast had begun but a cup of 'Cambodian Tea' would help stave off the hunger pangs for a little while so I found my moto and we went for a drink. The moto riders always take you to their favoured establishments, almost certainly because they get fed for the favour. As we arrived at the line of stalls the knowledge of this common arrangement didn't stop a small throng of girls with menus chasing us. "Mistaar, mistaar, you want breakfast? You want drink?" As soon as I sat down the first of the many children that come to the table to hawk cards and trinkets was waiting. "You buy my cards?" "I'm sorry but I don't want any cards today." "You buy my cards later?" "No not later." "You buy ten cards if I can tell you the capital of your country?" I knew that he would be able to name the capital city for any Nationality who visited Angkor Wat; it's one of the kid's specialities here. He was cute as a button though so I offered him a different contest. "You ask me what is the capital of any country and if I can't tell you then I'll buy ten cards, OK?" "Finland?" he said going straight to the point. "Helsinki!" "Poland?" "Warsaw!" "New Zealand?" "Wellington!" I said with confident ease. "Madagascar?" "Eeerm, erm, Victoria!" "ah haah!" "What is it then?" testing him. "I don't have to tell you. You have to buy my cards." "Smarty pants" I said, handing over one dollar. If you ever feel broody this is not a place to come, as the children are just adorable. I was just finishing my pot of tea when a kid of about six came to the table with the earnest look of a City of London financier to broker a deal on a brass elephant. I didn't want one but gave him a little folding cash instead and jumped on the moto lest I be there all day with them. We headed for probably my favourite of all temples, Ta Prohm.

An Angkor Wat sunrise is big on the list; this morning's was my third. The hush it can command in a big crowd waiting for the sunrise is something else but somehow Ta Prohm is more dramatic. Of all the major temples this is closest to what the early French adventurers found; a huge stone structure in the muscular grip of the jungle. Deliberately un-restored it's a treat that even shared with plenty of other tourists remains exciting and mysterious. Huge rainforest trees literally grow out of the structures and cover the carved architecture with monstrous tentacle roots like frightening creatures. It's the stuff of a 'Boys Own' story or the scene for a Hollywood adventure blockbuster. In fact it's been both.

I had done my small tour and seen my favourites; I just sat and watched the tourists from the cool shade of an ancient doorway. It was late morning now and the heat was building, coach parties of intense Japanese, chattering Americans and giggling Taiwanese came and sweltered as earnest tour guides explained the history for them and for me. The British came and generally sauntered as if it were a garden centre on a Sunday afternoon or somewhere we might have conquered if we hadn't been busy somewhere else. Then just as my petty prejudices were coming out to play a very beautiful English lady stood beside me and showed her little boy the fantastic view I'd been enjoying. He let out a 'famous Five' wow! Before skipping off. It was a nice thought that a childhood memory of such majesty

had been fused in his neurons. A recollection of something spectacular to last a lifetime and into a future where sights like these will surely be scarce.

Outside the main gate my moto boy found me and I asked to go back to my guesthouse. Leaving the temples behind to lie down in the midday heat felt as decadent as taking a small nibble from a Savoy Truffle but I enjoyed the luxury.

14 Angkor Twilight

It was a moment that I'd hoped to keep till the twilight of my years. I awoke in the grip of the Alien. It had my lower intestine in a clenched fist and was twisting. It was waking me to show me what it could do. I smelt an awful waft of the geriatric ward, of incontinent old men and the shame. I stood in the shower the tears mingling with the spray. It was a sorry state. I was hungry and for a moment I wanted to go home. Pride picked me up. I laundered the evidence and got a grip. I had booked my moto to come back at

four to find a sunset and decided to go to Angkor Wat for the sundowner.

The fresh air was good and forest road in the low sun was beautiful. It was nice to know that these giants in the Angkor environs are as safe as any tree can be in Cambodia. Angkor Wat is surrounded by a moat 200 metres wide and the lush green was intense in its reflection. By the banks couples sat and in the water wading birds made long white streaks on the surface.

At the entrance the usual hubbub of hawkers called out. A small throng of boys played football on the ancient paving and I felt a small pang of guilt for a little bit of fun that got out of hand last time I was here. A kid of about thirteen tried to blaggard me and demanded I gave him ten dollars. I asked him why and squaring up to me, said, "Because I'm a gangster." With a sarcasm that completely went over his head I said "ten dollars? No. How about I buy you and the gang a new football and a Man U strip to go with it?" Believing that they'd hooked a sugar daddy the boys were all over me asking for even more and with every request I raised the anti in a mad upward hyperbole. By the time we'd finished there were bikes and all sorts on the list. I then asked for calm and said that I'd see them later. They acquiesced and we were afforded much respect. The following day at another temple a kid came up to me and said, "you're Ken aren't you? Can I have a football?" Word was out. Fortunately we split town the next day. I did think the leader would be a good fifteen, sixteen by now and maybe armed.

I stood in the entrance archway looking down the long paved concourse to the main temple building. I remembered how it caught my breath that first morning on the edge of dawn. It cheered me immensely and I was glad I came again this afternoon. As at Ta Prohm I had no need to explore, only to savour. I climbed the impossibly steep steps to the third and top level and found a window ledge to sit and watch the world. I shared the corner with a monk in his orange robes. We were happy to also share the silence.

Improbably we were joined, as it turned out, by an animated German guy who had lived in my home town for ten years which, he had just left to come travelling. I've nearly come to expect these kinds of meetings though his German roots added an interesting twist. "Y-yes, I w-orked with special needs people in Brighton " he said purposefully avoiding any hint of a 'Ya and Va', "but the place was run by less-bee-andz" he said in phonetics, contorting his mouth for emphasis. "I mean I don't mind less-bee-andz but it was a little bit st-range being the only man." His brush eyebrows seemed to have a life of their own. "Now I've got a job to go to in L-ow-zz teaching English. I mean in Brighton every body is just inter-estid in the latest Der-ugs. Its so boring." He engaged the monk in conversation, which went surprisingly well, he grasped the phonetics really quickly. The German needed plenty of space to talk, waving his arms around in big erratic arcs like a mad professor we were beginning to be pinned on the corner ledge. I began to imagine a deathly plummet and decided to leave them to it. I took a slow walk back, stopping along the way to feel the warmth in the sandstone and to appreciate the detail. Then just as I was leaving I was granted a small miracle. At the grand entrance a small group of children were at play like they might have played at anytime in history since Angkor Wat was built. Ragged-clothed but lost in their fun. The good travellers god had sucked up every tourist and for a moment left it untouched.

Back at the guesthouse I realised I wanted something as close to home as possible. In Phnom Penh my room had a TV, a fridge and aircon. I had my books and music there. The bathroom was bright and fresh. Maybe there was email from Bunty waiting. I wanted to tell Sena that I was going to head back but his phone was switched off. He'd be back in Phnom Penh by Tuesday and I'd talk to him in the meantime I reasoned with myself. I booked a coach ticket for seven but I knew the Alien would wake me before then.

The coach journey back to PP the next morning was easy. Much of the highway is still without tarmac but it was comfort. I did feel sorry though looking out the window for the motos in our dusty wake, but at least I knew how it felt. We stopped for lunch in Kompon Thom. I had had quite an education since I was here less than a week ago. It had been a big circuit of the North West and also an extensive tour of my emotions. It was a day and a half since I'd eaten and my resolve left me. I joined a table of other travellers and ordered a plate of vegetable noodles. The restaurant was filled with two coach loads of travellers waiting to be fed. I waited and salivated but my lunch never came. The bus tooted its impending departure and another traveller who hadn't got hers either threw a noisy strop. I was able to be more philosophical; at least I hadn't broken my fast. I enjoyed the calm it seemed to bring.

From Kompon Thom to PP the road is metalled and the flat landscape flashed by, it was good to be back among familiar sights. As the bus edged its way into the Central Market and the throng of moto drivers closed in on a busload of fares I was pleased that I knew where I was going. I grabbed my pack and pushed past the slick boys with good English and high fares and disappeared into a side street to find an honest moto.

EDUCATING RITA

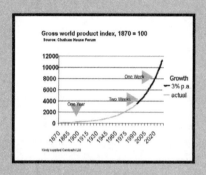

"One years World output at the dawn

of the Twentieth Century is delivered

in two weeks today. By the end of the

next decade it will take just one week.

Environmentalists would find this a

matter of concern..."

Cambashi Seminar 2001.

15 Fast Track

It was day three of my fast and I sensed victory. I had the upper hand in the fight with the organism in my belly; the struggling was nearly over but I had to make sure it was dead. Instead of a raging hunger I felt incredibly light and content, in fact I was aware how easy it had become to go without food. By now I would have expected to be stripping paper off the wall and devouring it like the hungry cows do on the streets of Calcutta. But instead I spent the day in the cool of my room thinking about what I'd seen.

The diet of cold clear water seemed to be clearing my mind and a startling new perspective was coursing through my head. In the last week I had witnessed the alarming speed at which the forest was being destroyed. I had been instilled with a sense of urgency and it was as if this rush had swept up all the particles of my inklings. They were settling into a new formation and a clearer view was emerging. A single line of thought was  plotting a route to something that was frightening and yet I was excited by the clarity. The logic seemed stable but I wondered if as a stoned man understanding the meaning of life I might lose it the moment I closed my eyes. Whether this hunger-induced understanding would evaporate with the first mouthful.

I felt sure that I wasn't the only one to see the simple line.

What I found scary therefore was the apparent lack of urgency to be found in the output of the Western News on the impending doom that seems to be upon us. While the folks back home were focused on the war in Iraq I had been reading articles in the Cambodian Daily that only now started to add up to something far more sinister than the fight on terror. We are the weapons of our own mass destruction.

It scared the shit out of me but the simple logic went something like this. The first world despite all the green gloss is consuming at an ever increasing speed everything the developing world can dig up, cut down or pump out for its own benefit. Despite having the party to ourselves we've decimated the forests and it's wildlife, killed whole swathes of the oceans and pumped enough CO2 into the atmosphere to change the climate forever and more. Though the buffet is still being devoured there are gatecrashers at the door. In 1999 the world's population hit Six Billion, in just over twenty-five years at current rates it will stand at Ten Billion.

While Mssrs. Bush and Blair posture on the war against terror the true terror stands behind the veil of distraction they call news. Work it out for yourself but to me it seems the only way to keep an extra four billion hungry hands off your party cake is overwhelming power. It will mean ensuring that it is in the hands of a few. You may be smug enough to think that you will be one of the chosen but as the shit begins to clog the blades who knows where the crap will stick. Perhaps the British computer technician trekking in the home of his ancestors, Pakistan, would hardly have believed that his holiday excursion warranted a term without trial in Guantanamo Bay. A regime under threat can be very paranoid.

This stuff I was reading wasn't something that's secret or hidden, it's there with the masses of other information that pours out at us every day. But in the half a dozen 'World' stories to be scanned in the Cambodian press each day I found a clarity I had missed in the deluge. For instance I read in the 'Daily Business news' that China had used half of the worlds' cement output and over a third of the world's steel for the month. That it plans to pipe oil in from Central Asia, an area once dominated by Russia, to fuel its ambitious expansion plans. The most populous country on the globe is at the bottom of a steep ramp of growth that will surely create intense competition for the raw materials of production. Western carmakers have earmarked Twelve Billion Dollars to establish manufacturing operations there, which will be producing Six Million units a year by 2007. India wants to be at the top table in less than twenty years; it's car sales were up forty percent on last year.

We have our futures pinned to growth. Our pensions, medical care, our children's futures and the value of our homes; all linked to a steady three percent a year minimum (India and China's economies are growing at more than double that). Three percent sounds like a nice cosy figure. Growth in the economy is presented as great news, the bigger the better. Stack it up year on year though and you have a nearly vertical spike of consumption that since the eighties has ravaged the environment and looks frighteningly unsustainable. How will the common quoted estimates of thirty years of oil left in the ground look when these new economies really get in the swing? What will happen to the forests of construction timber or the wildlife that used to call them home? Why don't our leaders tell us there's a problem? Surely someone's briefed them on the situation.

I wondered who would elect a candidate on the 'Reality' ticket? Perhaps it's rational not to talk about it; after all we've all seen what can happen when the market gets the jitters. Millions can get wiped off the value of the markets on just the whisper of something dodgy. Growth can turn into decline and our homes can be worth less than we owe on them before we even realise the boom just came to a halt. Best keep our mouths shut but make sure that when the lights start to go out that we've got the biggest gun. I guess that's what George and Tony have in mind.

I wanted to hang onto this clarity but feared I was fast becoming the kind of bloke to be found with a sandwich board traipsing the streets of London predicting the end of the world. Maybe I should eat.

16 Rita

I was ready for a big breakfast but I knew I had to be careful after nearly four days. Having made the decision to start eating again my stomach felt as big as a hanger. My favourite place was the little Indian restaurant across the road. They served a beautiful and simple breakfast of dhal and chapattis, which I had with a banana lassi. It tasted like an Ashram breakfast and the association made me cheerful. I was ready to plan another trip. Sena wasn't back till tomorrow so I decided to go back to the UN Library and look at some of the books I'd skimmed last time. Perhaps I would find more about forest dwellers and Spirit Trees.

The helpful Librarian remembered me and left me to it. I pulled out a pile of books and settled in. The United Nations Development Programme has a mission to eradicate human poverty and although there were still whisperings of doom in my head the positivity of their ambitions lifted me out of the dark space I had inhabited the day before. Whilst I still felt there was realism in my thoughts I was happy to wash in the hope contained in their objectives. I was really moved by the forewords to the UNDP reports, I had expected to read corporate fluff but instead I found the very human qualities of compassion and an overwhelming desire to do better for the poor of the world.

As I read more though I wondered how they manage to remain optimistic in the face of such a task. The statistics are pretty astonishing. The 2003 report states that more than fifty nations grew poorer in the last decade and the inequality gap grew still larger. Interestingly the gap between the rich and poor in Cambodia and the United States is statistically nearly the same; whilst the richest 20% have roughly 47% of the wealth the poorest 20% have just 5%. If things are getting worse then the 1998 UNDP report on the consumption of resources by the First world and Poor countries seems even starker. Globally, the 20% of the world's people in the highest-income countries account for 86% of total private consumption expenditures - the poorest 20% a minuscule 1.3%. More specifically, the richest fifth consume 46% of all meat and fish, the poorest fifth 5%. The rich consume 58% of the total energy output, the poorest fifth less than 4%. They have 74% of all telephone lines, the poorest fifth 1.5%. Consume 84% of all paper, the poorest fifth 1.1%. And own 87% of the world's vehicle fleet, the poorest fifth less than 1%.

I guess we all like to think that when we buy something that comes from a poor country we're helping to lift them out of their miserable conditions but it's clear that it doesn't quite work like that. I read a report on the value of timber exports from Cambodia conducted by a US Auditing company. It said that the trade in 1997 should have delivered $100 Million Dollars in tax revenue but the treasury saw just $12 million; the rest presumably disappeared into the pockets of the corrupt power brokers.

As I sat reading, engrossed in all these facts I began to realise that something was happening to me; even if it was only the library, a working class bloke at the UN? I had to smile to myself, after all I spent most of my working life as a hairdresser and this was close as it gets to an 'Educating Rita' moment. In the film the Rita character, a fluffy suburban hairdresser finds culture through evening classes in literature. Her stiff intellectual English lecturer Frank, played by Michael Caine is beguiled by her innocent passion and sets out to nurture the scrappy little flower. All is fine while Rita knows her place but as she blooms and starts to find her voice he becomes threatened.

I wondered if I'd be threatening now I'd caught the evangelical passion of the newly converted. I wanted to tell people that one American consumes as much energy as forty-one Bangladeshis and that fifteen percent of the world's population consumes nearly sixty percent of the world's energy. I had the power of knowledge. I knew that this was scary stuff because I could even hear my own defence mechanisms whirring. I'd read the papers and seen the images on TV; I'm as good as the next man at putting bad news in boxes.

I wasn't sure what I was going to do with it all but somehow I felt I had a right to be there, maybe five hundred kilometres on a moto had given me permission to question why these things were going on. Perhaps it was just that I'd seen first hand what these statistics look like in the real world. I wondered if that's what it takes to become an expert, to change a traveller into an activist? Blimey.

17 A New Guide

I'd been very fortunate to land a trip with Sena but if I were to be able to fulfil my desire to see a Spirit Forest or head off into the forest on my terms then I would need to find my own guide. My first attempt had not been so successful but hopefully now I was clearer about my objectives I would be better able to steer the project.

Sena had given me another contact and I had got replies from emails I'd sent before we went off to Preah Veah. A lady from the Forest Network had written and had offered assistance up North in Ratanakiri though no-one was available for another week and there was a question mark on the following week as the Khmer New Year's celebrations were approaching.

I set up a meeting with Sena's contact a guy called Phal, roughly pronounced Paul. I told him that I was keen to see Spirit Trees and meet with Forest Dwellers. He seemed really enthusiastic and his English was pretty good too. Sena had suggested Kompon Thma an area closer to Phnom Penh in the Province of Kompon Thom as a starting point. He said that there were still people living in the forests nearby, though a new rubber plantation was bringing about rapid change in the surrounding villages. The notion of fewer travelling days appealed. Phal said he knew the area very well and could take me into the forest. He wasn't cheap though and something unidentified nagged at me but as I made "I'll think about it" noises he very nearly begged. I didn't have much choice either if I wanted to be off again soon so I put aside my doubts and made plans to leave in two days.

In the meantime I decided to carry on library hopping. I was beginning to find holes in the information. I guessed that as the Khmer Rouge had destroyed most of the libraries that had existed pre 1975 most of what's on the shelves today has been created since and mostly in the last ten years. For instance I couldn't even find an encyclopaedia on Cambodian wildlife. Much of what's on the shelves is published by NGOs and issue based. As such the range of information is skewed towards academic research of those issues rather than the broader interests. Some of it is still fascinating but it was frustrating that the some of the basic information that we take for granted about our own culture and natural history just doesn't exist there. One of the things I thought was actually quite cool was the way that you don't judge a book by its cover in Cambodia. I began to lose my habitual way of judging before reading, as some of the better stuff was umpteenth generation photo-copied and bound with a plastic strip.

A database search at the Cambodia Development Research Institute produced a little bit on Spirit Trees by a Buddhist Monk. He documented how Monks in Cambodia are taking the lead from a Thai Monk and Ordaining trees to protect them. This must be why I'd seen some trees with Orange sashes. Also there was reference to a protest by villagers who had taken on the loggers cutting down their resin trees. It sounded like a small but very significant victory for the people versus big business. I noticed that the village mentioned Tum Ar was close to where Phal and I were heading in a couple of days so I thought I'd read more.

The Development Institute published a working paper on the subject of resin trees. People who live in or by the forest depend on it for all sorts of resources. What it doesn't supply they trade for with things they find there. It's the great provider for millions of people in Cambodia. One of the things referred to as 'Non Timber Forest Products' (NTFP), is a resin mainly collected from two evergreen trees the Chhoeuteal and Trach. The resin has all sorts of uses from waterproofing boats and making torches to paint and varnish production; it's a living for over 100,000 people in Cambodia. Until now these trees have not been subject to intensive logging as they're regarded a second grade timber. Now as luxury grade timbers become scarce loggers are focusing on resin trees and an ancient way of life is under threat. Despite a new law announced by the Prime Minister to protect these trees the chainsaw drivers are still at it; the resin collectors along with spirits it seems are the last line in the defence of the forest. I was keen to meet ordinary people challenging the likes of the businessman in PBY.

NO TREES, NO RAIN

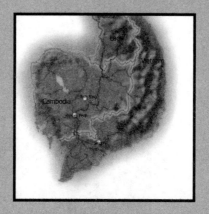

Eighty-five percent of Cambodian people

live a rural existence and roughly the same

percentage rely on natural resources to

support their livelihoods. Together, the great

lake of Tonle Sap and the forests are the great

providers. Since 1985 Cambodia's forest cover

has diminished from seventy-five percent to less

than thirty. The great lake is getting shallow.

18 The Road To Tum Ring

I found Phal my guide pacing about the lobby. As he caught me coming down the stairs he threw his hands up like I'd been a lost man. "Oh I was so worried you might have forgotten me. I went to the other hotel down the road to make sure I had the right place." He said holding his head. "But Phal, we said we'd meet at seven!" "I know but I came at six-thirty just in case." What I'd taken for earnest enthusiasm for my project was I realised actually the behaviour of an obsessive. The nagging doubts that I couldn't quite put my finger on the other day came ringing in. I couldn't believe what he was wearing either, we were off to the jungle but he was dressed for a breakfast meeting. He had a clean crisp shirt, a briefcase in one hand and a mobile in the other

– an immaculate model of pre-millennium man. "I have brought my car to go to the taxi." He said sweeping open the door. "Why don't we just go on a moto?" I said, puzzled. "Oh no, it will be much more comfortable." I didn't quite see the logic but there was nothing to do.

At the central market Phal dropped me off at the taxi stand while he went to take his car home. I wondered whether he'd change into something more appropriate for the road but when he returned he'd just substituted his case for a locally made Louis Vuitton bag. The display of affluence only pushed up the cost of the share taxi to Kompon Thma our jumping off point for Tum Ring.

He asked if I would pay extra to ensure there were just three people in the rear - he didn't want to get crumpled. Reluctantly, I agreed the comfort tax and we were ready to go when a couple of girls crammed in with the driver. Now there were four in the front of the compact saloon. Phal squirmed and tutted at the last minute additions, "this is very dangerous, can I ask one of them to join us in the back here?" I just ignored him and wondered at my judgment.

We wallowed out of town on knackered shock absorbers while the driver hung on the horn as we dodged motos, ox-carts and heavily laden trucks billowing black diesel. The Khmer Highway Code favours the fast or quick-witted and as a passenger I've found it's best not to look. Beyond the Boeng Trabek lake Phnom Penh City peters out and an 'out of town' commercial strip takes over. There were gaudy signs for the large beer garden restaurants popular with middle income Cambodians. They promised excitement and James Bond'esque women. It reminded me of India and I thought of Bunty and briefly wondered what the hell I was doing.

Phal had made himself comfortable and managed to command a majority stake in the rear seat by spreading his legs. He chatted to the pretty girl beside him while his posture grew with her every titter. I descended into a foul mood. I didn't like myself for it but at least character assassination took my mind off my poor choice of guide. I disgusted at his long cultivated pinky nail, symbol of the idle rich in societies where to work with the hand is to  be poor. The fake 'Hugo Boss' belt and mobile phone cradled in his crotch like a mauve phallus. He was wearing semi-mirrored wrap sunglasses. What would simple farmers and forest people make of us? We'd be as odd as Spock and Capt. Kirk in Babylon I imagined.

We stopped for breakfast at a reasonable looking Coach Stop. As we got out of the taxi a kid with a tray of glistening cooked spiders thrust her wares under my nose. Their black hairy bodies piled high in what smelt like a sauce of diesel. "Mmm… Not for me" I said moving quickly onward. As usual there wasn't much for the vegetarian so while Phal lifted the lid and poked his nose into the line of saucepans I brought some fruit from one of the vendors outside. They had some crusty bread to dunk in my sweet milky coffee so I was content with my own continental breakfast. Phal rapidly sucked and slurped his way through his assorted dishes and we were off again.

I recognised the road from the trip up with Sena not much more than a week ago; then whilst I had had no idea what I was in for I at least felt confident that Sena knew what he was doing. This was shaping up to be something altogether more of a mystery tour. We passed a new pagoda under construction; the monks had kept the pond outside filled and a splash of colour from the water lilies reminded me of the lushness of monsoon when they're in bloom all along the roadside. Phal asked me what I thought about the new pagodas being built. He said that he thought it would be better if they built schools instead. "People here don't go to the Pagoda, so they spend all this money and then they are empty." I had to agree but suggested that we could all benefit from a bit of the Buddha's loving Kindness. Then felt immediately guilty for my unkind thoughts towards Phal.

We arrived in Kompon Thma, a nice enough rural town, deposited our bags with a pick-up bus and looked for lunch. We picked our way through the mess of the market in the midday sun. Many of the established stallholders swung in hammocks in the shade leaving the desperate to sit it out in the open, their produce withering or stinking in the heat. I emptied my pockets of small bills for the sad collection of beggars, there was no stream of tourists to help out here.

At the back of the market Phal steered us to a surprisingly good restaurant, cool and substantial and made from strong red timber, a floor of big flagstones. I decided to make the most of it; I was learning to grasp the opportunities for a good meal when they were presented. This was clearly Phal's established philosophy as he woofed down another few plates. He ordered some bottled water and though I knew only too well, he lectured me on the dangers of un-sanitary water, lettuce and ice. It sounded like an announcement to a group of tour bus tourists.

I was beginning to wonder if that's where most of his work came from. He got stuck on the subject, with tales of this kind of bug and that kind of lurgie but it all seemed more than good advice; hygiene was another thing to obsess about. Even here at the hint of dust he covered his plate with one hand and pinched his nostrils closed with the other. He had allergies to dust, he said. The small warning bell was now a clanger.

Before we got on the pick-up he suggested we got some supplies, "there may not be any food in the village for you." His solution was a 24-packet box of dried chicken noodle. "I'm vegetarian", I said. "Oh, don't worry, just chicken flavour." With out much of an alternative I gave in. "Yes, if it comes to it you can just eat these for breakfast, lunch and dinner", he chortled. Though he seemed to find it very funny I lost my sense of humour and compassion all of a sudden. I engineered a small and spiteful come-upance. I occupied one of the cab seats and filled the spare with my bag forcing Phal to ride in the back. I avoided his little pleading look and sadistically assigned him to the un-hygienic conditions of the rear. A vegetarian scorned.

19 Into The Forest

Not far out of town we joined the forest road. For ten miles or so it cut through the giants in a red strip. There was plenty of evidence of logging but still choice trees lined our way. I clicked away with my camera as the driver enthusiastically pointed out the great old hulks. It was over all too soon though and the light flooded through the windscreen as if someone had thrown the switch on the back projection. Before us was the wide-open space of Tum Ring Plantation its border the ancient forest now ripped and exposed. It looked vulnerable.

The village sign read 'Khaos'; it seemed apt. The place looked like it had been ravaged. This was the dormitory village for the plantation workers. A wide strip of dirt and a string of low timber houses, which, if viewed in black and white would look like a gold rush town of the 1900's. Phal had survived the dust and even gone up in my estimation by distributing some of my dried noodles to a hungry child though was it possible that I detected crumbs in the lap of his trousers? We sat beside the dirt crossroads under the one and only remnant of the forest that must have stood there. I braved a lurid coloured crushed ice and tinned milk drink from the vendor who'd set up stall. She flirted unashamedly with me to the whoops of a few local boys who'd come to stare at us. I wondered whether this was the start of another case of the shits or if the Preah Veah Cocktail had toughened up my system. Was I mad?

Clearly Phal didn't know what was next. He asked if I wanted to see if we could stay at the Police Station; it certainly didn't appeal. There was no evidence of a guesthouse or even a wide boy on a moto with a deal. This was the end of the line for the bus too. The bus boy skulked over to see what we were doing and said we could stay at his brothers if we liked. Without any other plan we piled our bags back onto the pick-up. Just a hundred yards from the ugly wide red road the old village tucked up to the forest, a reminder of times gone.

His brother had a little store and welcomed us by clearing some space for our bags and dusting down a couple of tree stump stools. It was a rattan and thatch structure with a little counter under a shade that doubled as a shutter at night. There was a stock of village essentials, goodies in a few jars and a cool box for the perishables and a little supply of beer. It looked very basic but I thought I could hack it. In fact it looked quite promising, the travellers angel had offered up something authentic. A few curious villagers came to take a look at the 'Barang' and the man in the city clothes but we were treated with quiet hospitality. The afternoon sun was dipping and we took a  walk through the village towards the edge of the forest. A villager with five or six well-fed cows sauntered along the shaded lane towards us and waved a cheerful hello. In the yard of a large village house three girls pounded rice; two seesawed a long beam that hammered the grain whilst the third redistributed the flour in the mortar between the heavy blows. It was a medieval scene.

At the end of the village the lane forked where the forest ended and the new plantation clearance begun. Leaving the cosy village I was unprepared for the shock. An apocalyptical vision of a burnt and flattened forest still smouldering, its blackened limbs and stumps seemingly caught in a last gesture of shock and disbelief. It made me think of the petrified figures at Pompeii. It was beyond my comprehension and I struggled to find even a question that might begin to explain how someone could do this for profit. Phal was clearly distressed too. We quietly stood together looking at the carnage, acres of charred soil and smoking wood. They were destroying the forest to plant neat rows of

77

rubber. Pathetic little seedlings strung out in lines where majestic rainforest once stood. I was in danger of losing it but what was I to do? I found myself shouting "fuckin Stoopid" sounding like Sena. It seemed to help.

I had to get the shocked black limbs out of my head and I thought maybe a cool wash down might restore my composure so we headed back to the village.

With the sun and temperature dropping the village had come to life. The little store had a queue of customers, children played and people were returning from a hot day's work. Around the village well a small throng were soaping up and scrubbing at the layer of red dust that starts to accumulate within minutes of the last wash.

I was wondering whether I was ready for public ablutions when Phal emerged from the back of the store wearing a fabulous pair of gold and blue 'Gucci' branded shorts. Clearly designed for a 1980's Greek Oil Magnate at least two feet taller than him, the waistband tucked comfortably into the fold above his belly and just beneath his nipples. It was the antidote to the horror up the lane and also my cue. Wearing a pair of orange "Thunderpants", novelty underwear I'd purchased in New Zealand I stepped out to join him. It was an absolutely free moment. A lifelong fashion victim and body conscious individual I stood amongst foreigners in bad pants and of course none of us could give a toss. The water from the well was as refreshing and luxurious as anything that could be devised by a western product development team and the chuckles of my companions were contagious. The crap of the day was rinsed away. I felt clear.

Phal's worries about the lack of food turned out to be unfounded and our hosts had cooked up a tasty meal for us, me a wholesome plate of veg and rice and something meaty for Phal to pick at. There was green tea to wash it down and we happily tucked in. In the fading light candles were lit and the smell of cooking wafted from the village homes clustered around us. Kids were still playing and puppies scampered about but the village was winding down. Before it was completely dark I decided to string up my hammock and mosquito net and lather on the repellent. I was not taking anti-malaria medication so I had to be cautious.

If I smoked I would have sparked up a big cigar just then and retired to my hammock but as Phal settled into telling Cambodian tales a small posse of police turned up. Obviously word that a 'Barang' was in town had reached the police chief and he popped down to take a look. A few words were exchanged about me, which seemed satisfy them and he and his boys sat down to a table hurriedly prepared by our hosts. A case of beer was produced with deference and we were invited to join.

Chief was relaxed at the head of the table and I massaged his ego a little with some questions that emphasised his importance hoping that he'd go as soon as he was satisfied. From what I'd heard about police corruption, I thought locals would be happier if we didn't have them hanging around. I didn't want them in our hair either. They settled in for a session though, there was beer to be drunk. The Chief talked of the so-called development in positive terms, the road, TVs, motos and the school which now had a teacher. "Malaria is a thing of the past since the forest's been cleared", he said through Phal acting as interpreter. I smiled, sat back and left the conversation. I couldn't go through the motions any longer; I was content enough to watch the body language and the faces in the half-light.

The police stayed till their beer was gone and left us with a tractor driver and his son who worked for the clearance company. He remembered the village before the plantation and talked about the changes. He said, "before we all ate together and we loved each other very much. Back then if you offered money or fruit for a chicken people from the village would get angry – we shared. Now they know the value, how much it costs. It's different now." He explained how villagers and outsiders were being given 3 hectares of plantation rubber per family. They will clear and tend their plots and when the rubber trees mature in three to five years sell the latex to the company. In the meantime they can grow crops between the young trees, though not rice. It sounded like a positive story to me but with little capital to tide them over he said poor families had already started to sell their plots for less than $100. I could see how back in Phnom Penh the Government would reap some great headlines for helping the poor by dishing out free land but in reality the Rubber Company was quietly snapping up the cleared and planted land for $30 a hectare. Bearing in mind that the luxury timber that once stood here sells for up to $1000 a square metre it all sounded like a neat and more than self-financing scheme.

Phal had given up interpreting and before slipping off to my hammock I stood in the lane to take a pee and look at the stars. Without the light pollution of the city the night sky is dazzling, it's a wonderful display that we're deprived of in the urban west. Layers of stars upon stars deeper and deeper into space, as close an illustration of infinity we'll ever have. As I slipped into sleep I had a momentary feeling of insecurity hanging as I was beneath the open shelter of our hosts lean-to but the sounds of the village were reassuring and I fell into a sound slumber.

20 No Shit

The village was already awake. My brain went into catch up as I watched from behind the security of my mosquito net like some nosy neighbour on morning life. The impending heat of the day makes a necessity of a dawn start and already field workers were heading off. Phal's stomach was his driving force and he paced around waiting to be fed. A bit reluctantly I engaged with the day stealing myself to become the centre of attention. We went down to the only place that served breakfast in the village.

Out on the crossroads strip there were a few vendors squatting on the ground cooking scraps on makeshift barbecues or selling rice and pork rolled in banana leaves. The workers' cafe looked rough and as we walked in I imagined a scene from a Wild West film where the honky-tonk piano stops and steely eyes meet. If there was any animosity though it was because we stood in the way of the TV that was belting out a Kung Fu movie in its thrilling 'beatem up' ending. As much as it jarred at that time of the morning at least the action from the corner was more interesting than us and we could eat in peace. The food was fresh and hot and I found myself gawping at the TV too and soon joined the conversation vacuum.

I wanted to meet forest people and suggested to Phal that we try and find resin tappers. I wanted to head off into the jungle but Phal had asked around and said that there was a family in the village that collected resin. I was introduced to a lady who launched into a rant about losing her trees. "Now we are poor and we must eat rice porridge", she said, but there was livestock in the yard and she looked far from starving. Perhaps she had taken me for a visiting charity worker and this was her rehearsed performance but it didn't seem genuine.

Phal looked at me with a bit of a lost look and I realised that I had to be more directive with him. His local knowledge was not what I had hoped for so I asked him to try and find someone to take us into the jungle. Another villager showed up willing to guide us and to at least show us some resin trees; perhaps we might find something. He was a fit and wiry old man with the knees out of his trousers and a battered old hat sporting a faded label that read 'love needs no excuses'.

Beyond the devastation we'd witnessed yesterday was the standing forest and adjoining it were the paddies of the old village. Our guide stopped to tend his palm trees and shimmied up and disappeared into the crowns swaying in the breeze. We sat in the dry paddy below; it was still green and made a pleasant lawn to admire an older way of existing within the forest. The small green clearing was beautifully harmonious. 'No excuses' climbed down with a good couple of litres of palm milk and we took a refreshing drink before heading on.

In the jungle there was a wide track rutted by vehicle use and from this thoroughfare numerous tracks into the denser stands. There were holes in the canopy everywhere and plenty of stumps and downed trees. It was on the way to becoming 'degraded forest' the next step on the path to becoming deemed not worth keeping or fighting for. Further from the plantation the damage was not so extensive and maybe left alone for 20 years or so it would regenerate itself.

We'd only been walking for a couple of hours but Phal was starting to look flushed, it was easy going but he called for a halt to rest and take lunch. I was happy with a few bananas but he'd got packets of the dried noodles. While we were resting he sent the guide on. He made it sound tough, "let him find some big trees, we must save our energy for the return trip." He said dabbing the sweat with his hanky. I was getting pissed off with being in Phal's comfort zone and descended into another 'black dog' of a mood. The crinkling of the noodle packet and Phal's munching on the dried contents stabbed at my impatience and unspoken discontent. I sat in a fog.

Small forest bees were attracted to the moisture on my skin and I watched them feeding off me, trustingly they gathered what they needed. They were either without sting or malice but they made me consider my own uncharitable feelings towards Phal and the deeper source of my frustration. This attitude, an example of my western thinking, 'I want my significant experience, and I want it now!' was just another form of consumerism. A very close cousin to what was destroying the forest. As Sena said, I had much to learn but in the meantime it didn't make sense to project my discontent onto Phal. 'No Excuses' had joined him in a meal of noodles out of the packet but their combined crunching did less to irritate me and they respectfully put the wrappings back in the bag rather than discard them here.

Our guide had found a nice tall Phdeak; luxury timber so surely doomed and a strong looking Chom Bak but little evidence of a viable resin tree community. We decided to head back. I was disappointed but I was trying to remain aware. And then just as I had come to terms with my unrealistic expectations we met a man coming along the track. Clearly at home in the forest and carrying a long handled axe he looked interesting, Phal stopped to talk.

He was a resin collector and on his way back to his village from Khaos where he's been to complain about losing one of his trees. It was just what I'd hoped for and we squatted down to listen to his story. Though Phal acted as interpreter Sek looked straight into my eyes as we talked; he seemed to be checking me out. I could be working for the Rubber Company, or the Concession loggers Colexim who despite officially having lost their cutting rights still seemed to have a say here. He searched my face as I looked into his. His looked both old and youthful at once, a life in the forest had toned his skinny little frame and a big smile covered worries that emerged anytime the grin muscles relaxed. We made a connection and the conversation flowed.

He said that his family had 500 trees but recently they had lost 50 to the cutters. He said that he would not sell his trees; they were his farm, his rice bowl and an inheritance from his ancestors. "We are poor people, simple people. They come to our village with guns and knives and we are afraid that if we are strong with them they will kill us." In a cone of green leaf he rolled and lit up some tobacco and settled into telling us all about what was going on. Above us birds were busily feasting on something and a light shower of seeds rained down on us. He told us how the

83

businessman named Mnong had tricked them. Ten days ago they had cut one of his trees and when he complained to the Tar Kong, the chainsaw drivers they said to talk to the Big Boss. When he complained to the Big Boss he said they were not his Tar Kong but offered Sek 10,000 real, $2.50c to compensate him for the loss. With little alternative Sek agreed to the compensation of two dollars and fifty cents but was told to come back tomorrow. He was still awaiting his pittance for a tree worth up to a thousand dollars, he said.

I asked him if he knew about the law that the Prime Minister announced the year before that forbids anyone to cut down a working Resin Tree. He said that only if the Colexim company and the Rangers agreed to help him could he do anything. I thought about the Rangers up North at the businessman's table. In truth no-one was going to help Sek. He agreed show us his trees and to take us to the remains of the one cut down just ten days ago. He was eager to guide us and we arranged to meet him the following morning at his village. We said goodbye but a few yards down the track Sek turned and called out; Phal interpreted, "please help us our situation is desperate." I was touched by his call but I wondered what I could do.

Out of the jungle the temperature was a few degrees higher and we stopped at a farmers shelter beside the paddies. It was a little raised platform with a grass roof and in a hammock a young woman breastfed her baby while grandmother watched over another young child. A playful young dog tried to engage a few scruffy chickens in a game around the cinders of the breakfast fire. It appeared to be the family of our guide and we flopped in the shade with them. An extra mat was rolled out for us and in minutes Phal was asleep.

There was a stream just close by and I wandered down to find a bucket and a washing area. Now an old hand at this kind of thing I stripped down for a rinse. Over-hanging trees provided a natural shaded bathroom where dragonflies darted above the water and tiny fish scattered to avoid being scooped up. The stream was moving jewellery. Inside this nature's cocoon I was insulated from the realities just a little way down the track. I knew at that moment this perfection would be a place I could return to, to summon heaven.

Refreshed I found that a little snack of cashew fruits was waiting for me picked from the tree that stood a few feet from the shelter. We smiled silent acknowledgements of friendship, I rummaged in my bag for some kind of gift but really none was expected or required from me. I imagined myself happily enjoying a kind of Tom Sawyer existence here. Hanging in the hammock watching the sun go down listening to the sounds of jungle in the warm evening air. Just then Phal stirred, probably his nagging appetite disturbing his rest. It was time to leave this little idyll and get back to the village.

On our way back Phal confided that it was twenty years since he'd walked so far. If I hadn't been high on the meeting with Sek or fresh from a beautiful experience with the family out by the paddies I might have gone for his throat; this was a man who'd represented himself as a guide with experience of the forest. Even so the irritation I'd felt for the last couple of days was beginning to drain away and though he'd bullshitted me it seemed to matter less.

I now had a delicate question for him. While it was obvious that it was permissible to take a leak pretty much anywhere with discretion it was not obvious where one took a shit. Fortunately my constitution had recovered but I was now in need. "Ah, it can be complicated", he said without elaborating. "There is a house in the village that has a toilet though. I will ask them if you can use it." He then cautioned that they were Muslim. I decided not to question his prejudice for now but I was interested to know what he was thinking all the same. The 'Muslim house' was one of the more substantial constructions at the edge of the old village and stood on solid hardwood stilts; I followed Phal in through the proper gate. Beneath the upstairs floor the lady of the house was stretched out on a day bed with her child. A momentary confirmation of my request was all it took for an older child to be sent to ensure that the facilities were ready for guests. By the time I emerged we'd been invited to stay.

21 Top Rankin Tum Ring

I felt a bit bad about upping sticks and moving out of the little store. The bill for food and lodging was miniscule so I covered my guilt by paying them double. Phal had booked dinner at the store even though we were moving into the Muslim house but when I questioned him about this he said that there were many mouths to feed there and it was better that we ate here. I asked him whether he'd informed them but he gestured that I shouldn't worry about it. I wondered what was going on in his head.

After dinner we left our hosts at the store and crossed the village to our new residence. Apart from the family a host of others stayed there, it was more a small community than a household. A common religion was the bond for young and old, farm worker and tinker, man, boy and girl. Nothing austere, strict or forbidding about life here, nothing of the representation of Muslim life that was currently scaring the crap out of western TV viewers. Phal was clearly enjoying himself chatting to everyone – he was so buzzed up that he had pretty much forgotten that he was my voice too. One of the young girls asked if we liked bingo and invited us to a game that was about to start in the back room of the 'general supplies' next door.

Maybe fifteen souls of all ages were sitting in the little stockroom excitedly waiting for the evening's entertainment. We all had to ante up a 100 real (a couple of pence) and the winner took the pot. Rather than sit left out I offered to 'call' with Phal as interpreter; it went down a storm. I did my very best Brighton Pier performance and though I'd long forgotten all but the classics I made up calls on the fly. I was in hysterics with my own inventions, which was obviously interpreted as mild madness by the others. They were quick to catch on with their favourites; "Number 1; muy, Two Little Ducks! M'phei pii, NnnnNineteen! Pram buen dAnd Ap. Soon the counters were going down to 'clicker d click and two fat ladies' before Phal had had chance to interpret and I had to tone down my more saucy calls for fear that my cockney rhyming slang would slip into common usage. Soon the room was packed with players, spectators and faces pressed in the windows and back door. I'd found a new talent and it was another moment of freedom.

The generator and the lights go out at ten o'clock at the Muslim house so at nine thirty and only 500 real down my performance ended for the night. I delighted the assembled with one final laugh by walking into the dwarf sized doorframe and stumbling out into the road.

If Phal had any idea that we had moved into comfort he was about to be disappointed. Not that our guests hadn't gone to some trouble in preparing our space. A mosquito net was hung out for us in the main room of the house, a few rich red boudoir like cushions were scattered underneath and a little lantern guarded the stairs but the floor was fearsomely hard, the planks cut into my hips and shoulder. The hardwood construction was now pouring out the heat it had stored up throughout the day and I lay in a sweat envious of those swinging in their hammocks outside.

Perhaps I was more tired or hardy than I had thought because I was soon in a lovely dreamy place when I woke up to my own shout and a stabbing in my feet; there was a commotion in the mosquito net. In the dark confusion I wondered if my hosts were intent on killing the infidel but then realised that a giggling girl was trying to retrieve a kitten that was anchored to my foot and wrapped up in the net. Having unravelled the poor thing I was now wide-awake and aware of all the house noises. One in particular will stay with me, that of the large gecko that lived in the eaves of the kitchen. Not the little choppy "tut tut tut" that anybody who's travelled anywhere around the Med or beyond will have heard but more the sound of a frog with a harelip calling through a bull horn "Gek Ko!" I drifted in and out of sleep for the rest of the night witnessing the dawn and the morning prayers to Allah and then just as the sun was coming up I fell into a coma. I awoke with a start to find that everyone was up or already leaving for work. I'd hardly had more than a few hours sleep and felt like a bag of poo.

22 Tar Kong

We headed straight for breakfast at the café on the strip with me still pulling on clothing. To his credit Phal had already arranged our transport for the day with a flying doctor of sorts, a former Khmer Rouge medic who travelled around on a battered old Korean motorbike dispensing shots to villagers. But Phal wasn't going anywhere without food

Another gangster movie piped through the kare-oke machine rattled the place but we knew now to come in behind the view of the screen so we hardly got a look. As we woofed down breakfast Phal said we should order up a pack lunch. I said I'd be happy with some fruit, which he took as some kind of threat, "I must have food!" he declared. I told him it was ok, ok to get something to take for lunch. I picked up a hand of bananas and we met up with our ride at the store. We had to be away lest Sek the resin tapper think we might not be coming.

The three of us squeezed onto the battered old seat and set off for Sek's village Rum Chek maybe an hour away. I was grateful for a cloudy morning as we set out across the unsheltered plantation to the forest. Clearance workers were hard at it scrubbing up stumps and raking at the remnants of vegetation, creating a featureless landscape. The bike squirmed in the loose sandy soil and 'Medic' stopped to rearrange us. The apparent problem was the positioning of the heavy Barang. I was to be moved to the middle and the centre of gravity. I protested that I was clearly not the heaviest here and offered up my belly for comparison. This the second sleight on my weight was not going to go unchallenged. There was some conversation between Medic and Phal, which might have qualified for a slot in the Royal Society New Years Lecture along the lines of the 'specific gravity of the European vis-à-vis the Asian belly'. I admitted defeat and took my position in the middle.

Though there was a vehicle track into the jungle the damage looked less extensive. The deep sand gave over to orange laterite, the volcanic rock that's the base material for the monuments of Angkor and the going got easier.

As we pulled into the village I quickly realised that we were the only the synthetic things in the place. Fortunately the dust had transformed Phal's designer attire but just as I had predicted we looked like Spock and Kirk surfing the coordinates. I was struck by the absolute simplicity of the village and yet how it looked far from impoverished. It was neat and well cared for, purposeful. There wasn't any plastic or brand names, any artificial colour beyond the faded clothing of the villagers. Sek was waiting for us and he beamed as we pulled up. Tea was brewed and he rolled a cone of tobacco and invited us to squat down. As we chatted a sinister looking guy buzzed through the village on a motorbike, "They know we're here," said Phal interpreting Sek's observation. The distant sound of chainsaws was clearly audible and I guessed the guy on the bike was making sure we weren't about to disturb their work.

Sek showed us his store of liquid resin and the rustic pots used for collecting it. He told of how it took days to get round his trees. He talked with pride. I was already in love with the way of life when Sek got on to hunting. He described how villagers created an impenetrable barrier in the forest to catch anything that tried to get through. I winced as he said that once they'd caught a tiger. It was a reminder that even in our perfect projections all is not how we want it to be.

Sek's trees were back down the track so 'Medic' transported us in a couple of trips. As we sat on a big log waiting for Phal and the Medic, Sek pointed in the direction of the chainsaws that were working close by. The sound was probably only a few hundred yards into the forest. The prospect of a confrontation with the loggers was scary but to ignore what was going on would be hypocritical. When Phal arrived I asked him to ask if Sek was up for going to check it out. Phal explained that Sek's trees were in the opposite direction and that the Medic wouldn't leave his bike as loggers had trashed it on a previous occasion. Phal clearly didn't want to go but Sek picked up on the conversation and appeared to be ready to follow the sound of the logging. "Let's take a look," I said and we started off down the track. Just a little way along in the thick of undergrowth Sek pointed to a big tree that had been cut down very recently. We were investigating when we heard a moto thrashing down the path towards us. Instinctively we all dropped into the cover as he rattled by. "The Medic must have told the look-out that we're coming to catch the chainsaws." Said Phal. "I don't think he saw us though." Back on the track Phal looked indecisive, I offered a rhetorical, "Shall we take a look?" and headed on. I was quietly crapping myself. Looking round I saw that Phal had dropped back and Sek was looking hesitant. The chainsaws were louder now and there was a good chance that we really might catch them at it. I rubbed my good luck stone and pressed on.

Over the din of the saws I hardly heard the motor of the lookout's bike coming round the corner; his face was like thunder. He flew past us and then did a smart U turn and sped back towards the chainsaws. There were shouts and the saws stopped. Now all was eerily quiet. Either they had run or were waiting for us. Sek was behind me now.

23 Pisson God

Like a bunch of kids caught smoking three guys stepped out of the trees onto the track and slipped by us. It wasn't what I'd expected and I half thought that perhaps these weren't our culprits. I walked on to see what had been occurring and found a couple of large trees; one clearly a Chhoeuteal resin tree, felled. Both had been largely processed into squared logs and much of the Chhoeuteal had already been transported away. Sek was visibly shaken; he sat down by the stump.

I went back to find Phal talking to the lookout. They were doing what Cambodians do, saving face. I was awash with adrenalin but they were making friends. I asked who he worked for and why they were cutting resin trees when it was against the law but Phal seemed to be moderating my temper. The lookout said they were cutting timber to build a house. It didn't ring true. My questioning seemed pointless so I went back to Sek who I realised was staying out of it. He looked scared and I understood why. He didn't want trouble; tomorrow he'd be on his own. We sat together and he talked to me in Khmer. Although I didn't understand him I used the counselling skills I learnt sometime ago, I just listened. Actually I picked

up quite a bit. He told me through signing that the logs were transported from here out to the main road and back towards Kompon Thma and that the Tar Kong came from Khaos. He showed me the tracks of ox cart that was used to get the squared logs out of the forest.

We found Phal and the Tar Kong sitting on the remains of the tree they'd been sawing up, chatting. This was not how it was supposed to be. I was angry and I was up for confrontation. Just like an angry man in the pub spoiling for a fight they avoided my eye. Phal said, "We've just been talking about the spirits" and smiled a placatory smile. The fight or flight chemicals were tumbling down to my boots and a flat swell of depression flooded in to take up the space. I listened to what sounded like a load of old tosh. Phal said, "The people here believe that there are good spirits and bad ones. Sometimes they will go to the Spirit House and say, 'Oh spirits, or Tak Nhom, the mountain spirit, please help me find food and I will offer you a chicken.' And the good spirit will help them and they come back from the mountains with lots of things but then they forget to give an offering to the spirits. So then the bad spirit will punish them and the people will get sick in the stomach or something like this. Then they must go with bananas or a chicken to the spirit house.

Now they say that the Spirits are getting weaker or that if you believe in the Jesus spirit then you can do anything. If you pray to that god then you can even piss on the spirit house and nothing can harm you." I asked to Phal, "do they think that the Jesus Sprit and the Tree Spirit are different?" He sought to clarify what I was asking and then said that the Tree Spirit was like Satan, was the opposite of God and that sometimes he would help you but also he would harm you. That if you prayed to the Jesus god then you would be able to protect yourself from the bad spirit. I said, "Tell them that the Jesus God and the Spirit God are the same." "The same?" "Yes, tell them that the Jesus God and the Satan God are the same as the Good Tree Spirit and the Bad Tree Spirit. They just have different names." This seemed to strike a cord and Phal smiled as he relayed this to the Tar Kong. They nodded as they considered the concept. Then I said, "Tell them, if they are the same god then if he believes in Jesus and pisses on the Spirit House then he is pissing on his own god." This got a round of acknowledgement. Then one of the guys started to explain something through Phal. "He said, his younger brother pissed on a spirit stone and the spirit must have been in there because he got sick and they had to take him to Phnom Penh for treatment." I said, "Tell them that's what happens if you piss on your own god!" Phal relayed this and they all laughed but I wanted to psyche them out for the next time they came to cut a tree. "Come on, its time to leave." I said and we walked back out to the track and the Medic.

I dug into the bag for water to find that Phal's lunch had seeped over the bottles; they stunk of greasy pork. Then I realised Phal had three lunches packed. This was a spark to light my fire. "For fuck's sake Phal you've got three lunches! Why do you need three" He swept the floor. "You better make sure you give one to Sek." "I already did, but he didn't want it." I watched him scoff down two lunches waiting for the opportunity to throttle him should we even consider touching the third. Then he swilled down best part of a litre of water. I quietly made plans to make the bastard walk a good deal further than yesterday on top of that belly full. The lookout came to join Phal and the Medic on one end of the log; Sek and I sat at the other. They chatted with the enemy and we sat in silence.

The two pork lunches were only just settling on the bottom when I said, "Right let's go." Phal asked Sek which way and he pointed straight into the undergrowth in front of us. "This is not possible for us Ken. This is very thick jungle there is no path. It's impossible. Maybe we can look at something else?" "No, I want to see Sek's trees and I'm sure he'll lead the way." I sounded like matron and it was the perfect retribution. Phal made one step in all directions, beside himself with the prospect, muttering and flustered. He rummaged in the bag and produced more water, which he took  a few large swigs out of. Then measuring it against my bottle said without much logic, "now we have the same." I gestured for Sek to lead the way and into the thicket we went.

He flicked at the dense growth with a billhook on a long handle. It was either fearsomely sharp or it was a knack developed over the years as it sliced through the vegetation with ease. The blade was a kind of jungle windscreen wiper flipped to the vertical, though Sek made it look like a stroll it was hot and hard going. Bring it on I thought, the pork in Phal's belly probably weighs half a hundredweight by now. There are all sorts of things to puncture and scratch you in this kind of jungle. Though it was darker I kept on my sunglasses to protect my eyes against the hanging vines with vicious spikes and stuff that makes the brambles at home look cuddly.

Sek turned to me and said, "An Teack!" and mimed for me to take a big step. I did what he said and carried on behind. Then a bit further on he gestured for me to stop and uttered 'An Teack' again. This time he carefully un-hooked a rusty wire snare hanging about shoulder height from a straining sapling bent to provide a powerful whip when the trip wire was broken. Ah, so that's what An Teack means. My survival instinct had just burnt that phrase into my neuro circuitry. My god it was like a Nam film in here I thought. This was no place for a suburban boy without a guide. Every now and again Sek would take a nick out of a tree to mark his way, it was featureless in its abundance.

We came to one of Sek's trees, a big Chhoeuteal about three feet across with a blackened hole in the front. Tapping the resin involves cutting a backward sloping hole in a large tree and briefly lighting a fire to stimulate the flow of resin, which is then collected after a few days. The hole grows as the tree gets bigger and the soot from the periodic fires creates a distinctive black mouth. They look like they might talk as a tree from the Wizard of Oz. This one already had a mouthful.

Further along Sek stopped to prod something with his billhook. It sounded like he was attacking a bee's nest but as I got closer I could see that it was a small deer covered in flies. It was black with them. I couldn't tell whether it had been trapped or not, but it must have been a recent death as there was no decay. The sound was amazing.

Phal was getting pink but my belligerence wasn't satisfied yet. Sek was keeping up a steady pace and I was finding it tough. I'd had a few smacks in the face from spiked foliage but there was no way I was out to slow things down. Then there was a crash behind me, I half expected to see Phal swinging by a snared foot but he was face down on the jungle floor wriggling to get himself out of a mess of creepers. He looked like a fat fish in a net and just as helpless. My bad spirit was satisfied and I went back to help. Fortunately we were close to the site of the tree that had been cut down just ten days ago. We sat amongst the butchered remains of a giant. All that was left behind was the debris from squaring the log and a substantial stump. We sat while Sek rolled up a cigarette. I asked where his tree went and he said that it went to Khaos village and then to Kompon Thma; that two men identified as Mhong and Mhow were behind the business and they lived in Khaos. He said that they had tricked him and not paid him any money for the tree. I asked him if they paid him how would he feel then. "I can't do anything to stop them. If they pay me then maybe I can buy rice." He was very subdued and there were long silences between questions. I asked if he thought the Forest was a beautiful or a hard place. "Beautiful." Then after a long silence he said, "Mr Mhow is a sick man, he has high blood pressure." "Tell him it's the spirits punishing him," I said to Phal. "Maybe." Said Sek. He finished his cigarette in silence.

We turned back. Phal shouted, "I've lost my sunglasses!" His precious designer mirrors were gone. I got the impression he wanted to send out a search party. His head dropped as we pushed on. Then incredibly a hundred yards on he shouted, "I've found them!" Holding up his glasses unmarked. In the dense thicket they'd offered themselves up. I said "the good spirits were looking after them for you." Then thought to myself, blimey maybe they were. Phal was as cheerful he'd been all day.

I was getting tired now but every now and then "An Teack" refocused me. Sek picked up something from the bush; the smell broadcast that it had been dead for a long while. It looked like some kind of squirrel but as he carried it bits fell off; it was in such a state of decomposition. But he clearly had plans for it. I was at the end of my water but I reckoned that we had at least one more bottle back with the Medic. We probably still had an hour to go and I tried not to think about thirst but just keep focused on Sek ahead. While Phal and I had guzzled our water Sek had hardly touched the bottle of cold tea hanging round his neck.

The buzzing of the flies around the deer approached and signalled that we didn't have too far to go. Sek deposited the stinking squirrel with the deer. He said he'd come back for them. Phal was clearly fascinated by the forest kill and talked to Sek at length about it. I wondered if he was just using it as an opportunity for a breather but I didn't mind. I wandered a short way and stood in the wonder of the forest. This was the real thing, a beautiful struggle to the light I thought. I felt I understood a little more.

At the track I said goodbye to Sek. I asked if I could come back and stay at his village if there was time before I left Cambodia. He was delighted by this prospect and I really meant it. And I still mean to one day. I gave him what I had in my pocket; it was about what the loggers had tricked him out of for his tree. It was so little I still feel ashamed to have not had more to give him but he unfolded his hand and beamed at me like I'd given him a pocket full of gold.

24 Desperately Speaking English

Sek went off down the track and the lump in my throat stuck on the dry wall of my gullet. I was choked and parched. I shuffled through the bottles to find all the water was gone. All that was left was Phal's remaining lunch pack and a hundred mil of porky wash back in the last bottle. I was thirsty enough to spill it down my throat, though I gagged on it. We hit the dusty trail home.

Back in the village I told Phal that I wanted to see the houses of the businessmen Mhong and Mhow. Phal went into another multi-directional shuffle and suggested that it wasn't a good idea. I said, "Its OK we can just ride past and I'll take a look, I want to know what kind of places these people have." I said to tell the Medic that he had one last job before he got paid. They went into a suspicious little conference. "You promise you won't take any pictures?" "No pictures, just ride me slowly past." I had my fingers crossed to tell a lie. "Ok then." We got on the bike and went up to the main strip and headed to the North end of the village. We slowed as we went past a reasonable looking house but it was nothing palatial. Phal elbowed me as a sign that this was it. Then Medic circled the parade ground of the disused army barracks opposite before stopping. "That was Mr Mhong's house," said Phal looking in the opposite direction as if at this very moment a powerful telescope was focused on his mouth and a trained lip reader interpreted his every word. "Now we'll go to see Mr Mhow's." This was more like Inspector Clouseau. We pottered by what was reputed to be Mr Mhow's place, a half finished construction with a couple of workers sitting outside who pointed at the Barang before the Medic swung back into the Muslim house yard. "OK?" "Sure" I said but they might as well have shown me anything and probably did.

I'd had enough of their game, paid the Medic and decided to be first for a wash. Outside the facilities was the well. It was as substantial as the village supply and a couple of lifts was sufficient to fill the plastic washroom drum for a plentiful slosh. I slightly missed being involved in the communal wash but the tiled room was fresh and clean and I did a proper job. A big bowl of chives stood by the window and I presumed that this was a natural insect repellant because even at mosquito prime time there were none to be seen. Bonus I thought. I admired the fact that maybe upwards of twenty people used this little room everyday and yet it was spik and span.

Underneath the house mother and one of the elder daughters were involved in a painful looking ablution. A good lathering of oil had been applied to her back, which the young girl scrapped off with the edge of a piece of wood. It left behind angry looking red stripes. What impressed me was that this was a Muslim family and I was a man in their midst but it didn't seem to matter that all this flesh was on show. Not that I gawped, I was keen to show that I was respectful of her privacy but it was nice that the atmosphere was so relaxed.

As I came down the steps dressed for the evening the workers were returning from the fields. The boys flew in the gate first, four up on a moto their hoes and picks in hand. The rider skilfully rode one handed while carrying a bright and shiny cassette player that blared a disco version of 'We Wish You a Merry Christmas.' The guys jumped off looking like a Thai Boy band dressed as farmhands. A giggling girlie foursome skidded in on their dust and did a little 'Jump down, turn around' routine before brushing themselves down like four brides for four brothers. Maybe it was a Friday night but even so this kind of exuberance was amazing after a good ten hours out there.

Though Phal had suggested that we try and find a Spirit Tree the following day I decided that I wanted to go back to Phnom Penh. There was still much to see here but I thought I would prefer to just hang out without the drain of a fifty-dollar a day guide to support. I couldn't really afford it for a long stretch. I was thinking that perhaps I would come back and stay at Rum Chek, Sek's Village to just observe the way of life and maybe find my own spirit trees.

It was still light so I thought I'd catch a bit of village flavour and walked out on my own. I popped over to the store for a beer and to watch the children play. I sat at my favourite stump. Lee the lady who ran the store was busy with evening business but cracked me a beer and filled a glass with ice. Her little boy and I had made a bit of a connection and he showed me his latest toys, a cardboard box and a stick. I remembered how much joy a cardboard box had brought me as a child and watched him fly and drive his with the same delight; imagination providing all the detail ever needed.

Phal joined me for a beer and we talked about the day and I told him that we'd be heading back tomorrow. He was OK with this, perhaps it was a relief, who knows but he was cheerful. "So" I said, "We're eating at the house tonight. You seem a bit worried about that." "Ah, well. Well you know Muslims are mainly fishermen and their houses smell of fish sauce. We usually think they are not very clean." "But Phal you eat fish sauce all the time and you know they're not dirty" "I know I'm wrong to think this, but I've never been in a Muslim house before." I was pleased that his prejudice was being dissolved.

Lee had a large washing up bowl full of live Catfish and there was a queue of customers waiting to buy them. Phal said, "There is a story that god asked all the creatures on earth who would be willing to feed the humans. He asked the Cow and she said that she only had one baby at a time and couldn't spare its life. He asked the Pig and asked the Chicken but they all said that their children were too precious. The he asked the Fish and the Fish said they were plentiful and because they loved God so much they would allow some of their own to be taken to feed the Humans. That's why the Fish don't cry out when you kill them you know."

I asked Phal about his time under the Khmer Rouge. He said that he had been old enough to work on the one of the labour teams. "Then you know I could count every bone in my body I was so thin. We only ever had rice porridge; we were starving. If we wanted more we had to hunt for it. Sometimes we would eat mice or even cat." "Did you eat dog like the Vietnamese?" I said. "Yes we sometimes ate dog too. Though you can only eat it in the cold months because it makes you very hot. But those were very hard times and I wouldn't eat those things now." "I know." I said. His three packed lunches explained. "They say at the Muslim house that it is OK to take some beer with our meal." He said. "Really?" "Yes, yes. They said it was OK." So we went back for dinner armed with a couple of bottles. The house was busy with freshly scrubbed extended family. Dad had made a fantastic contraption to pump water. He had attached a belt to the real wheel of a static bicycle, which was connected to a pump. He was grinning from ear to ear and peddling furiously to display the pretty impressive flow it was capable of delivering. It seemed a poor cousin to the well but our applause cheered him on for one final spurt. Then he got off and patted the saddle like it was a thoroughbred.

I sat on the day bed waiting for the call for dinner. Manysor introduced himself and came to join me. He spoke faltering English but with great determination, it was painful but he was desperate to converse with me. I persevered and hung on his every word as they came intermittently. After every half a dozen or so I would replay them so we didn't get lost. He told me how he had a basket and pointed to his bicycle with a basket of plastic household goods and toys on the back. This was how he and his father made a living, cycling from one remote village to another hawking their wares. The combined stock was probably worth little more than a few dollars. The he asked me how old I was and I told him I was fifty, "haasep." He searched for the words, and then launched into a question that I couldn't work out even though we went over and over it. He just kept staring with a pleading look repeating his question. Phal came by and I asked him to help. They conversed for a moment and Phal interpreted. He said, "Manysor was asking what the life expectancy is in your country. He wanted to tell you that if you were a Cambodian you probably would only have another few years to live!" Manysor was well beyond 'Hello what's your name' in his thinking but stuck on book one English conversation. I asked him to wait. I had an English / Khmer phrase book that I thought he could make good use of and besides I could get another when I got back to Phnom Penh. He was ecstatic and asked me to sign it as a good friend. I was more than happy to oblige. Dinner was called.

In the kitchen a large low circular table had been laid for the men. I sat next to Manysor and the man next to him was introduced as Manysor's dad. His dad had the most delicious smile and I was surrounded by food to match. There was an array of interesting vegetable dishes and a kind of omelette that was especially for me. Phal was beside himself, "This is the first time in my life I have eaten Muslim food! It's really good" He went back for spoonful after spoonful. Long after we had all pushed back Phal was still in there tucking it away. Our host graciously waved at the remaining fare and gestured for him to finish it all. I smiled to myself and thought, Phal would be going home with a whole new set of experiences and we'd all been his guides.

Hanging on the kitchen door my Bingo companions were keen to get their eyes down for another full house. Jollied by a couple of beers I was ready to really large it up. I was escorted into the packed storeroom, my place was prepared; they were ready for the Housey Housey Messiah!

25 Thunder

I lay awake. A breeze flickered the lamp on the top of the steps and in the deep blue rectangle of the doorframe the night sky was changing. Clouds scudded across in a hurry and the palms brushed the roof. The Gecko shouted in the kitchen. The first flash of lightning projected a momentary vision of a frightening monochromic world onto our secure interior. Though it's timing was uncertain the impending thunder was sure. In the limbo I felt the weight of my own prophecies. The clap made me jump the after rumble disturbed me.

I slipped out from beneath my net and sat on the top step in the doorway and watched the storm over the forest. It was beautiful. The rain was not here yet but the cooling wind was refreshing. I thought about Sek and what the future held for his way of life. I wondered what I might return with that could help them. His village needed little that might be bought in the City. They just needed to be left alone just as the forest must be protected.

A big fat splat of rain hit my foot and then another hit the step. A volley of luscious blobs showered down on the village clanging and crashing on the roofs like bullets. Then in less than a minute it stopped. The warm scent of the soil begged for more but there was to be none. The forest spirit kept it for itself.

26 Miss U Scarecrow

It was a 'Dorothy' moment from the Wizard. The balloon was waiting but I wanted to tell them all how I'd miss them. 'The Scarecrow', Sek, wasn't there but I knew I'd miss him the most. I ran down to the store and brought a big bag full of sweets for the children and then jumped on the pick-up before I made my spotty handkerchief all wet.

Locals had said. 'No trees, no rain' and as we left the clearing behind and joined the forest road the margin of last nights rain was clearly defined. It said cut down the trees and you won't get any rain in the most graphical way. The red road from here was fresh, damp and dust free. Scores of cyclists were out and clearly riding for pleasure like a Victorian England. We stopped every now and then to pick up little clutches of people heading into town all looking cheerful. It was the rain! Like the sunshine in England transforms an introverted nation into a smiling gregarious bunch here the first shower brings everyone out.

Sek's tree came this way just ten days ago on it's way to Kompon Thma and I wondered what happened to it. Something struck me. I had the names of the men responsible for cutting it down. It's more than we ever we get at home. Like it just happens mysteriously that a chunk of the Amazon forest the size of Belgium disappears every year, or that we're told that our biggest challenge is to preserve the world's rainforests without any information as to how we begin to meet the test. It's in the hands of somebody else. Why do they tell us if they don't give us the means to effect change. It's distraction news surely. Well Mr Mhong and Mr Mhow are up to no good and that's a start. Maybe this was the way to help Sek. Find his tree and shut down the business that stole it.

EDUCATING RITA PART TWO

The thing about Rita in the film was that for

a while she got sucked into thinking that an

education was all the knowledge she needed.

It was the end. We all smiled at the conclusion

though as she realised her literary tutoring was

little but a series of lessons on how others had

successfully revealed their inner truths. Simple

truth is all there is, it's there to find.

27 Slueth in PP

Back in Phnom Penh I said goodbye to Phal. We'd both learned a lot but I wasn't about to spoil a cheerful farewell with the details of just how he'd helped me. It's that old saying that you learn more from your foes than your friends. Phal had irritated the hell out of me; he pushed my buttons and in doing so brought out a petty strain of intolerance. I had projected much of my anger at what was happening to the forest onto him and of course he didn't deserve it. I knew I wouldn't use him again but we parted with a warm handshake. I imagined that his wife would have his lunch on the table and would set to those dusty shirts straight away. Order and a perfect crease would return to his life.

I was heading for creature comforts too. Friends of friends had kindly offered to put me up and of all things had cooked me the ultimate comfort food; vegetable lasagne. I fell into the bosom of western carbohydrate, red wine and air conditioning. I decided to give myself a day off from reality and blissed out on Cambodian herb.

Monday I was back on the case and went down to check my mail and to try and make an appointment with one of the most effective environmental campaigning groups in Cambodia, Global Witness. I had a tantalising mail from my contact at the Forest Network; she said they had a guide who could show me Spirit Forests in Ratanakiri though by Thursday things would grind to a halt for Khmer New Year. The New Year celebrations hadn't really come into my equation but now people were telling me that much of the transport network would either cease to operate or rocket in price. Ratanakiri was a good two-day overland pick-up ride away and that's if I could get on one first thing in the morning. Whilst a back-to-back trip didn't appeal if I didn't move now I would languish in Phnom Penh for best part of a week. I wouldn't even be able to work on Sek's case as everything looked like it was going to be shut. I wondered if there was a flight.

I spoke to Mike at Global Witness and he said he could spare me a little time later so in the meantime I went down to see if there was a flight up country the next day. The Travel Agent laughed, though then sympathetically offered to see if she could buy a ticket on the black market for me. She said that sometimes it was also possible to pay for a ticket and turn up and hope you could get on. I said I'd think about it and went off to my meeting with Mike.

There's no signage just an anonymous high green gate and a hand painted number. Global Witness makes no proclamation of their presence and with good reason. Flicking through the press here most weeks you'll find an outspoken comment by them on the conduct of one or other of the logging vested interests. They're certainly not popular with some businessmen and are a constant thorn in the side of corrupt officials. They're saying the things that need to be said but they're mindful of the environment they work in. It can be dangerous work.

I told Mike I was keen to do my little bit and about what I'd seen at Khaos and Tum Ring. Though it was obviously a situation he was aware of he was happy to explain in detail the business going on in the district and who was involved. The destination for much of the timber from Tum Ring is The Kingwood Company Plywood Factory. It hides behind high walls and unmarked gates beside the highway up to Kompong Thom. It's likely that Sek's tree ended up there. We had driven past it the day before I realised.

Mike gave me a historical overview of the situation to put the Kingwood Company business into context. In 1995 the forests were carved up into logging concessions. All the forested land of Cambodia except National Parks was parcelled up and awarded to logging companies and the military.

It was all done secretly and unconstitutionally but it ensured there was plenty of money to keep the military sweet. Despite a logging export ban announced in 1996 the trade paid for the coup d'etat in 1997 and Hun Sen's Cambodian Peoples Party (CPP) election victory in 1998. The military have long been involved in logging in fact Pol Pot and the Khmer Rouge financed their war against the Cambodian Government during the 1990s with timber sold to Thai Generals; they were reported to be making between ten and twenty Million dollars a month! All sides though have used the forests as their private bank account ensuring continued misery for the people and wreaking havoc on the environment. Massive illegal activity continued up until 2002 with the logging companies switching their focus to plywood production within Cambodia, as exporting got trickier.

The current government is theoretically a coalition with power shared between CPP Prime Minister Hun Sen and National Assembly President Norodom Ranariddh of the Royalist Party Funcinpec. However the playboy prince is viewed in many circles as Hun Sen's poodle and Hun Sen is acknowledged as the defacto leader. The Prime Minister, a former Khmer Rouge cadre has been widely acknowledged as being involved in corrupt dealing. His friends and family have been very successful in winning logging concessions. Global Witness was also responsible for releasing a secret document with his signature authorising a major illegal logging deal with the Thai military contravening the ban. Everyone knows he's in on it.

Along with other pressure groups GW, as they refer to themselves, have been successful in bringing about an end to concession logging but the cease-fire is very fragile. What I observed a couple of days before is part of the continuing guerrilla activity that's still ripping apart the forest.

Wondering whether Mhong and Mhow might crop up I asked who was involved in the business at Kingwood? Mike laughed, "it's like a dark comedy." Slowly and precisely he went on to explain how the logging interests fist fitted neatly into the political glove. "The woman responsible for much of timber business in the Tum Ring area and a large part of the input for Kingwood is Seng Keang. She's the wife of Hun Sen's cousin, timber baron Hun Chouch. Her business partner is another timber baron Khun Thong. Thong is both the brother-in-law of Minister for Agriculture, Forestry and Fisheries Chan Sarun, and also the father-in-law of Director of the Forest Administration, Ty Sokhun." It's a family tree that keeps politics, money and business in the Hun Sen lineage I thought. Clearly my culprits were so far down the food chain they were not far off amoeba.

"So what about the Kingwood Company, where do they sell their products?" "It's very dark too" said Mike. "Their main product is flooring for Shipping Containers. They're one of the leading players in that market. We haven't been able to find out much more as they seem to sell direct to wholesalers in China; there's no big customer we can name and shame. It's a very shady business inhabited by gangsters." He explained that they recently flew over the place at low level to see what was going on and discovered that there were still logs, almost certainly from Tum Ring, stacked up in the yard ready for the plywood manufacture.

Mike told me that Kingswood was part of a much bigger picture. Millions of dollars worth of logging business had been going on until very recently. In fact there was a stack of evidence to show that the rules were still being broken. "What happened to it all?" I asked. "It's been leaving the country in all directions. There are well-established routes out to Thailand, up through Laos to China and lots has been going to Vietnam to feed the garden furniture business there."

I had to ask, "Cambodia gets loads of money from the West in aid so why don't we say clean up your act or you don't get any more?" "Well the donors from time to time do make noises about withholding money but the Cambodian government is good at playing that game." The current moratorium on the big logging companies was a good example he explained. "They've called a halt to logging but the concessions are still in place and the companies haven't gone home." I couldn't believe that the donors were that naive. "Surely we should demand more of the organisations that give out the money?" It was clear the situation was something he had to work with rather than rant about and I admired the way he kept cool enough to explain further. "You have to realise that Cambodia is one of the older post conflict countries. It's low down the order of importance in the world view and as such it's the first step on the ladder in the career of most people working for the donor organisations. They have an agenda, which dictates that they grant money. Not to grant money is not to fulfil their function and it looks bad on their CV."

"This is crazy." I said. Mike paused for a moment; readjusting his professional composure. "Oh it's crazy for sure. Every one or two years the government and the donors get together for the government to make a request for aid. Last time the donors got tough and stipulated that there must be greater accountability and new controls on corruption. There were plenty of tough words but then after the posturing was done they pledged more money than the Government had even asked for!" I asked how much, "Oh, one point five Billion." Gob smacked I asked "What about the reforms?" Mike gave me the same 'you have much to learn' look that Sena introduced me to up in Preah Veah. I felt deflated "So the tapper I met near Khaos doesn't really have much chance of justice does he?" Mike's colleague who just walked in heard my rhetorical question and said "If the policeman steals your car who you gonna call?" They smiled sympathetically and offered to help if they could but for now they had to get on. It was enough for me too.

I went back to the apartment and paced about and then decided I'd try and get to Ratanakiri.

28 Party P.People

In my mailbox I had an invitation from Sena to a party he was having that night. I gave him a call to tell him that I'd like to go but I had plans to go to Ratanakiri at stupid o'clock in the morning so maybe I'd best give it a miss. He asked if I had a ticket for a pick-up and asked if I knew that Khmer New Year was coming. "Ken, you do know that everything will stop by Thursday?" "I know Sena, that's why I have to get on the case in the morning. I think I might be able to see a Spirit Forest if I can go tomorrow." If I'm honest I was whining and hoping that Sena might come up with an easy solution; he rose to it. "Listen, why don't you come to my house before the party starts and we can talk about it?"

I got a moto out to Sena's house near the airport. I found him sitting under a shade from the late afternoon sun with a couple of friends drinking beer. The party preparations were in full swing, a giggling production line of girls was chopping food under the veranda. "This is my wife and these are some of the girls who stay at my house. I have forty girls who live here." I had to confirm what he just said. "You have forty girls living here? Is this your personal harem?" I joked. "Don't be silly they are not here to have sex with me." Sena's mates sniggered. "They all work at the textile factory down the road. You see I have built these houses and they live here." Sena pointed to the low accommodation. It looked solid but personal privacy would have been limited at ten to a dorm. "They each pay me a dollar a week." I said that everything looked brightly decorated for the party. "Yes. Everyone will be leaving to go home to their families for the holiday so we are having our party tonight."

I told Sena that I wanted to go up to Ratanakiri to see a Spirit Forest there and that I had thought about flying up before the New Year properly got under way. Going by pick-up would probably only leave a day with the guide but I could hang out and see what happened after that. "Do you want to fly?" "Yes but the tickets are sold out. Everybody's heading North for the holiday break." I said. "OK. Do you want me to guide you? I can get Airline tickets." "Sena that would be fantastic." Sena's wife was watching the proceedings closely and I sensed that guiding me over the holidays was going to cause a ripple or two on the domestic front. "I have to talk to my wife first but I think she will agree. You will pay my expenses?" "Of course." She was clearly not happy about it but Sena gave her a full on charm assault. She shrugged and he turned and smiled. "OK, I'll make a call or two." He was only gone long enough for his mates and I to struggle through a few basic friendly exchanges. "We have tickets and we go tomorrow!" "How did you do that?" "Oh, a businessman buys all the spare tickets and then sells them to people who fly with no luggage so that he can freight goods. You just need to know who to call. I also checked to see about pick-ups but the price was already thirty dollars and you would need to stop overnight somewhere so it makes the price nearly the same" I was already up for flying, bouncing around in the back of a pick-up for two days didn't appeal. Though I would have to overcome my fear of flying Khmer stylie.

With the trip agreed we helped shift around the tables and tied up balloons, threaded streamers and generally got in the way. The food preparation was done and the girls were glamming up for the evening. Sena checked the Karaoke, which was to ensure that it met the full distortion level required of all machines in S.E. Asia. He belted out an unrequited love song or two; all was ready.

As the sun went down and with all the party people lining the yard Sena took the mike and welcomed everyone and introduced the guests, Sena's two mates and me. The opening dance was a circle procession of the yard in the Khmer style. It was simple enough that even I could manage an approximation without looking a complete tit. Basically it's a swinging two-steps forward with a little step to the side and back whilst twirling the hands in the 'King and I' style. We progressed in a stately wave. I grinned uncontrollably. The buffet was laid out and as guest of honour I was hustled to the front of the queue. It was all delicious. I sat with Sena's four-year-old daughter. She was as cute as a button and

I clinked her orange drink in a cheers! Which she took up with a sweet regularity lifting her glass and cheering me in between mouthfuls. Soon there were forty exuberant teenagers waiting to lift a glass in a 'cheers' too. It quickly became a drinking contest. I didn't stand a chance as beer after beer was thrust into my hand. With every contest I was tied with another friendship string knotted with a hundred Riel. I was festooned with so much small cash I was a fire hazard. The only safe place was the procession that had restarted and I took a few millimetres off my sandals avoiding the certain oblivion in taking on the rest of 'em. I was happily wobbling along looking like I'd walked into box of flypaper when I was flushed from that refuge by one of Sena's mates, "This is Rat's sister, your moto rider to Preah Veah. She likes you, maybe she can be your wife for the evening?"

In a moment of good fortune I was whisked off for another group photo and I seized the opportunity to get my head back together. I was in danger of falling off the back of my moto home and I still had to pack. I decided it was time to split before all was lost in a haze. I found Sena who looked remarkably fresh. "Are we still up for tomorrow?"

I said thinking he was bound to have changed his mind. "Sure. The flight is at ten fifteen. Meet me at the airport at nine forty-five. Do you have enough cash?" "Yep, I think so, but I can always get more at the airport."

I flopped on a moto back into the city. The breeze that fluttered my Riel cleared my head and I watched the night streets blur by.

GREEN GEM

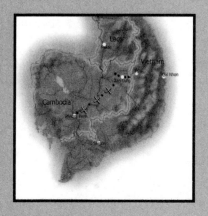

Ratanakiri is known if anything for its association with a Hollywood movie. Of dark jungle and primitive people bearing arms and the occasional severed head. In reality it's the home of Cambodia's hill tribe people and some of the largest tracts of the county's remaining forest. If I was to find my Spirit Tree experience I was heading in the right direction; I was on my way I thought, that's until Sena's bag went through the X Ray machine...

29 Patches

I don't like cricket! Ooh no … I thrashed about in semi delirium. I was Gulliver pegged to a jungle floor. My captors tormented me with the '10cc' chart hit from the Seventies. It poured into my ears from a long pipe, the sound mixed with hot oil. The Lilliputians must be intent on some form of mind control … Ooh no! I returned to consciousness from a bizarre dream induced by the combination of 70's pop, a belly full of beer and the thin cotton friendship bands that secured a couple of thousand Riel to my person. The green light on the clock registered zero four thirty and the aircon was off. Kerry and her friends were back from clubbing and still up for partying. I lay around till I was sure that all trace of the lunatic dream had left me and got up to be sociable.

Judging by the uncoordinated dancing going on in the lounge I guessed they'd be falling down soon so I went to make some tea. When I returned the boys had collapsed and the seventies classics had given over to something more ambient. It was cool out on the balcony and at least I wouldn't be late for the flight. We chatted till dawn.

Completely unlike me I arrived early at the airport and found the check-ins for the two airlines that depart for Ban Lung, Ratanakiri every other day just opening. I sat down opposite the entrance to be sure to not miss Sena. The minutes ticked on. A mild concern started to set in as the queues for the check-in swelled and then diminished to just latecomers. I started to wonder if I was in the right terminal. I asked if I was on either of the passenger lists. No, but these were the only flights to Ban Lung. There was still no sign of Sena and the first flight was due out in fifteen minutes.

I started to run around like a mad thing. I needed a telephone; my mobile wouldn't connect to his. "I must have a phone!" I demanded of an airport official who looked at me as if I were demented. I found a phone outside the terminal but Sena was engaged. I ran around some more as the final call was announced.

My phone rang, Sena was saying, "where are you?" And then like a cheesy phone ad we were in the same crowd. He said, "Just stand here." He went upstairs with a hundred dollars and came back waving a pair of blank tickets that the guy at the check-in wrote our names on. He scrubbed another couple off the passenger list and wrote us in. Then in a bizarre procedure he gave us the tickets, which we were to give to him, which he gave back to us less the flight voucher. Fortunately I hadn't had time to think about the condition of the plane.

Calm now we waited in line to be searched. I laughed at my panic. As if it really mattered. I tried to imagine though the real panic of those hoping to be aboard the last flights from here in April 1975 perhaps on the day the Khmer Rouge marched into Phnom Penh. Those who didn't make it out would surely have perished.

Our stuff went through the x-ray together. There was a discussion about something on the screen. Sena was instructed to open his bag. The official pulled out what appeared to be a slim handle of some description and gave it a shake, then a close look. Sena jumped in quickly to demonstrate that it was a flick-knife lest the thing engage in the face of the guard. He flushed with embarrassment and then continued to watch his bag empty of its contents: two mobile phones, one walkie-talkie, a GPS device, a Dictaphone, video and digital cameras. "Any other weapons?" "No", said Sena. "We'll return your knife at the other end," said the guard impassively packing it all back. "Do you think we'll be needing weapons then Sena?" I said sarcastically. He looked sheepish.

It was free seating so we grabbed window views. The Russian pilot garbled something and we were off. From the air Cambodia is virtually without concrete development and not much more than dust for half an hour out of Phnom Penh. We crossed the mighty Mekong twice, first over Kompong Chum, not far from Sek's forest and then again near Kratie where rare fresh water dolphins are still to be found. Reassuringly thick forest cover began on the fringes of Monulkiri province and covered much of our approach into Ratanakiri and Ban Lung it's provincial capital.

The green broke and the red dirt of the airport and town came into view. Ah, I hadn't imagined a dirt airstrip. The undercarriage lowered for landing to reveal two badly worn tyres on my side of the plane. Swathes of rubber had been worn away to expose the canvass carcass. You'd judge them dangerous on a bicycle. I took a few pictures that might benefit the crash investigators and gave my good luck stone a rub. But we were down, the dust kicked up in the turbulence.

With the dust settling again our fellow passengers walked towards the small wooden building that was the airport, Sena said, "this way's quicker," and we cut across the runway and into town through the huts and low housing lining the airstrip.

30 KaChun

Ban Lung is a scruffy place that seems to fit the provincial capital template; a couple of main roads converging on a circular concrete monument with its mythical Naga snakeheads smacked about by traffic. It could have easily been Tbeng Meanchay capital of Preah Veah. There's a growing tourist trade because of a few local gems so there's a couple of reasonable hotels and a few places to eat but otherwise it's the same scruffy nowhere's ville.

The one thing that would have been useful was a bank. In the panic at the airport I forgot to draw out some more money and a quick calculation left me well short. I foresaw a major hiccup but Sena said he could get money sent to him at very short notice and not to worry. Mr fixit came to the rescue again.

We rented a chunky 250cc trail bike and headed off to the forest. We travelled in sprung comfort and I imagined how much easier the trip up to Preah Veah would have been on one of these. Sena shouted, "this is a great bike what about I see if it's for sale and we can ride it back to Phnom Penh?" "Why not!?" From the first big hill outside town it was possible to see the forest stretching out towards Laos. Plumes of smoke dotted our route to Voen Sai thirty-five kilometres away on the border of the Virachey National Park. I started to feel the anger rising. All along the road it was the familiar sight of smouldering and flattened forest. I yearned for a landscape undamaged.

A fat tree with a sash stopped us. He towered above the rest and we had to pull up to admire him. As I followed the trunk down to ground level I caught a strange face in the undergrowth. It was a figure in a mask. I was wide eyed till I realised it was an effigy. I tugged Sena to look, he said, "It's a Chunchiet cemetery, you want to take a look?" He explained that the Tompuen tribe bury their dead in the jungle and make an effigy of the deceased to stand by the grave. Amongst the trees and undergrowth brightly painted little houses for the dead await the onslaught of the jungle. Their owners stand at the corner decorated with a symbol of their status in life. On one grave a man wears an army cap and carries a walkie-talkie.

As well formed, as they were I wonder if he'd have presented himself for parade with his genitals exposed? There were a few newer brightly painted carvings but the jungle had got to work quickly on the gaudy paintwork peeling it away to the bare wood; the cracks in the wood created an eerie detail. A faded sign read 'Please don't take photographs' but with no one around I grabbed a few choice shots.

While the dead rested undisturbed the forest 100 yards further on burned.

On the outskirts of Voen Sai we stopped to stretch and pulled up by the banks of the Tonle San River. It was a beautiful spot and we sat among ancient mango trees. Sena said, "this place belongs to the Hero concession and was about to be logged but the villagers made a big protest. They saved it for a little while." We looked out onto the Virachay National park across the wide strip of water. I said, " At least that place is safe." "Sorry Ken but the Loggers have been at work there too. Though it's supposedly protected there's no actual law to say that its illegal to log in a National Park." Nothing is safe I thought, there are just varying degrees of security and this cool and fragrant spot was hanging on by its fingertips.

Voen Sai reminded me of Southern Laos and I wasn't wrong. Sena told me the community is a mixture of minority people, Lao and Chinese. It's quite different. At the boat landing there were a few stalls selling snacks and drinks. The use of plastic bags to serve up the fare was a bit of disaster as shredded polythene hung in the bushes and drifted up against the side of the road. I walked down to take a picture of the river but the litter was nasty. We had our Slushies served in a glass. Away from the landing the village was tidy and there was plenty of tree cover to provide an intimacy that was appealing. A big painted sign over the main road appeared to extend a welcome and displayed a feeling of civic pride missing in Bang Lung.

We were on our way back to town, it was late afternoon and I wanted to make some time to really plan how we were going to spend our days here. We buzzed along the hard surfaced road, without the need to scan the road for holes I drifted into another place. The low sun flashed intermittently in my face through the holes in the canopy. Without really knowing where it came from I told Sena to stop. I told him that I'd like to look in the forest. He looked puzzled, "what here?" "Yeh. Please." He shrugged and turned down a small track. It was good for fifty yards and then we had to walk. I preferred the quiet anyway. Sena was keen to show me the fruits and medicine that could be obtained from this tree and that but though I was more than interested I wanted to be silent. Like a puppy with a boring master he gave me up and went off in search of more interesting things. I walked slowly and thoughtfully though I wasn't aware of any particular pattern of thought. I was just finding the small details fascinating, the shape of leaves and the colour of the light on foliage. The small path opened to an area of cleared forest. Sena was taking pictures of everything like a forensic investigator at the scene of a murder. "This is all very new. Look the sap is still seeping out of this  stump and here look the leaves from the crown of the tree are only just wilting. This tree has just been cut." The body was gone;

the log had been dragged away scraping its way to whatever carried it off. Sena went in search of more new evidence leaving me to sit and look at the remains.

I squatted down and went into another zone. Not aware but clearly aware. It was like the feeling I'd felt in the Kauri Forest in New Zealand with the Lord of the Forest, 'Te Matua Ngahere'. There were no big trees here though, the stump before me oozing its amber resinous sap was probably the last big tree in this patch. Beside me was a bent old Chom Bak hanging onto a young untapped Chhoeuteal for support, they were the last of anything substantial. We were friends at a funeral. The presence of the departed was still strong and the clearing felt like forest alive with the sounds and vibrancy of the creatures that had lived here amongst the branches and soul of the trees. It was strangely beautiful.

Sena came back with reports of more logging but there were still some big trees to see and invited me to go and look. I said, "Look how that Chhoeuteal is holding up the old Chom Bak. Its kind of brotherly." Sena caught my mood and looked at the pair for a minute. "No Ken. The Chom Bak is protecting the other tree. The Chom Bak is a spirit tree and they won't cut it till last. While the old tree embraces it the Chhoeuteal it will be safe." "Where do you think it will go, the tree cut here?" "Probably where its brothers and sisters went. To Vietnam." He gave me a look I remembered from Preah Veah temple when I got upset about the wildlife trade. "Come on let's get back." He shoved his arm round my shoulder, "What do you want to do?" "I want to find out what happened to the brothers and sisters," I said.

31 Slash N Save

I stood in the shower lost in my thoughts about the tree on its way to Vietnam when Sena shouted through the door. "Hey Ken, I just met an old friend of mine. He works here for an NGO. I told him that you were interested in Spirit Trees. He can help you, lets go and join him for a beer."

Graeme said, "Ah so you're the spirit tree man!" Though it sounded pretty eccentric like I might be the kind of bloke to wear socks with my sandals it had a nice ring to it. "Yep, that's me." Then Sena added, "Ken's a very sweet man." Graeme smiled and nodded a 'bless him' look in the direction of Sena. "Blimey, let's get the beers in!" I said moving a clunky introduction on. Graeme had the look of someone who'd seen a bit of life, a craggy Aussie with British tendencies, easy going whilst suffering no fools. Sena piped up "We got some great pictures at a Chunchiet Cemetery earlier." "Really, you're not supposed to take photos" said Graeme. I said "Yeh they've got a sign up saying not to take pictures but right next door they're burning down the forest. Its crazy." Graeme looked me straight in the eye and quietly said, "That's because they would rather not have their dead disturbed and next door they're practicing their swidden farming techniques. It's not crazy, it makes perfect sense." He smiled very generously and made sure that his direct response was understood, it was no more than putting me straight. I liked him immediately.

"So what do you want to see and do while you're up here?" I told him that I really wanted to see a spirit forest and then without a thought "I want to follow a tree to Vietnam." "What do you mean?" I tried to explain what I really hadn't yet worked out for myself. Without a skill to give or a job with an NGO to define my purpose I had to create my own. I wanted to bear witness to what was happening. If I could find the tree that got cut down where we were today and go with it I might be able to do something. Tell people at least. Graeme seemed to take me for at least a genuine eccentric. "Well look I can help with the Spirit Trees.

I work with a Kreung village and they have a Spirit Forest that you can see. I'll give Sena the details and you can go and see the Chief in the morning." Whoosh, just like that I thought.

We went across the road and joined a multinational bunch of NGO workers for dinner. They were all friendly but they recognised the maniac that was poking out the side of my smile. For them the holidays were nearly here and the troubles of the world would be there in the morning. They wanted beer and a good dinner. Graeme on the other hand was not the kind of guy to switch off and I jumped on his willingness to talk about the forest and what's happening to the fabric of the communities. Sena was basking in his celebrity status, clearly he was well known in the NGO fraternity even up here. So I engaged Graeme in a question and answer session. "So tell me about Swidden Farming then. Is that what all this burning is for?" It was a bit of a loaded question but Graeme didn't bite. "OK. I'll tell you about Swidden Agriculture and then we'll talk about the burning." He knew the argument well. He explained that forest dwelling people around the world have used Swidden techniques since ancient times. "It's a very efficient way of growing when land is plenty and labour is short." "But clearly that's not the balance now." I jumped in. "No, now things are out of control but the blame is not with tribal people. They believe that if you look after the soil everything will be well."

Graeme was passionate about his work with indigenous people and it was important to him that I understood the distinction between the destruction and swidden. He explained, in swidden the farmer will clear an area of forest by simply burning it but this isn't Slash and Burn and isn't about trashing the soil. Without disturbing the earth with a plough crops are planted between the stumps. The soil is only used for one or two crops before they move onto another plot. This may sound wasteful but because they don't disturb the soil too much the seedlings and other new growth that have been waiting for the chance burst into life. The surrounding forest will very rapidly encroach and within twelve years a young open forest will provide an area for wildlife to live and thrive. "Animals actually prefer this kind of forest, as it's easier for them to move around and it supports an amazingly diverse range of species." He was in a groove now and I was soaking it up as a willing pupil. He told me how the village works as a community and that all this activity is carefully controlled; each family is only allowed to clear what they need. Plots are cleared in strict rotation to make sure the soil isn't over worked and no old-growth forest is cleared only previously used fallow forest. "So you see it's actually quite healthy." "I wish I'd known that a month ago. Seeing the forest ablaze everywhere has done my head in." "You've come at probably the worst time for burning." "This isn't all swidden though is it" I said. "No, I'm afraid what you've been seeing is mainly land grabbing." Graeme's mood changed, it was as if he'd been in the good old days but now I was asking him to go somewhere else. "The old social systems have been bypassed and the new ones are corrupt." Even now left alone indigenous peoples maintained the borders of their communal areas and protected the surrounding forest. Their impact on the environment was really low but unfettered exploitation by outsiders was ripping communities apart. The problem he explained was that there was no law beyond the laws of opportunism. Wealthy people mainly from Phnom Penh were exploiting the lack of land law and governance by simply taking it. Forest where communities had lived for generations was being forcibly claimed and the people that lived on it were being evicted. The whole system had been upset and a horrible extension of the logic of ownership threatened the existence of the forest; jungle by definition belongs to no one and the only way to demonstrate that it belongs to you is to clear it. Now there was a double bind. Businessmen were claiming or clearing jungle for agribusiness schemes, which in turn displaced indigenous peoples. Those displaced from their cultural lands were moving to other parts of the jungle but to establish their rights to stay were forced to clear it. "It's out of control and the situation has been accelerating at an alarming pace. The last six months have been really bad. It's hard to imagine that there'll be anything left of the forest outside the park for much longer. And to top it all there's talk of the old Hero Concession up by the Viet border starting up again." They were using the 'terrorist threat' as an excuse to remove forest cover along the frontier, he told me. "You're right to be angry about the burning but don't blame the minorities, they're just the scapegoats."

"Hey you guys, that's enough of that. Come and join our conversation." Said one of our dinner buddies. I gave Graeme a nod of thanks and we joined the mixture of gossip and politics. It was good distraction.

Later as we said our goodbyes Sena and I got invited to a party for the following evening. As we crossed the street, Hanna shouted "we'll be having 'North Sea Oil. Leave your head at home!" Sena said "it's her special Norwegian drink."

Sena and I were dorming together and picking up from Graeme's observations he tried to embark on a lengthy and complicated explanation of Cambodian politics on top of half a dozen brown ales. It was tofu. I had something to say though, "Sena, thanks for giving up your holiday time off to do this. I really appreciate it." "Ken, we're Brothers in this thing you know." He said and gave in to the fatigue and stout by flopping on his bed.

32 Spirit Lights

As I slipped into sleep I went back to the clearing and the bent Chom Bak, I was happy to let go. Standing together in the half-light the tree told me of another time. "Ah yes I remember a different dawn, before the days of fear. The lights of my brothers and sisters would dance above the canopy and our spirits swirled and played in a vaporous display, mixing with the One. A human with the eyes to see it might have mistaken the rich blues and golds for Celestial Lights.

It was a time that I now remember with longing. A time when the first light brought the chattering whoop of the Gibbon and the calls of the long-tailed black bird the Kam Trong KanTrei; when the life on my bows beeped and buzzed its myriad rhythmical sounds, flashed its miracle beauty in a thousand ways and organised its multitude communities in common purpose without the notion of 'I' or the unfulfilled hunger of greed.

Then I was straight and tall, a Chom Bak, connecting the heaven to the earth with the universal force of Neak Ta the guardian and guiding spirit that lives in all creatures. A force felt in the longing of the heart of the human and understood in the nature of others as the procession and purpose of our re-creation. It was a time when our family of forest was so rich with spirits that we would play games with the people that came to us, tempting them to see beyond the shrouds of fear that blind them; assaulting them with beauty. The wings of a hundred dragonflies in a spear of light, the heady scent of Champa or a haunting bird song.

Now our spirits are scattered and I am old and bent. I'm one of the last. I have watched the fear of the human destroy the family of forest. First came the soldiers to take my brothers and sisters to buy the guns to kill their own brothers and sisters for fear. Hardness had taken them and they didn't hear our wisdom or see the beauty that could have saved them. Then came the Tar Kong, the chainsaw drivers, servants of the rich and lost. In them we smelt fear but theirs was of Neak Ta itself. They tried to appease the Chom Bak by placing the head of an ox at my base, its blood seeped into my veins and we cried at their ignorance. Even now we tried to reach out but the beauty frightened them more. They cut and burned and left the ones like me they feared most to bear witness, the Chom Bak."

Dawn seeped in under the door and through the fanlight. Sena stirred but I pretended to be asleep. I needed time to savour my dream to piece it together for longer-term storage, longer than my tree's dawns perhaps.

At breakfast in the market I was back on the bananas and French bread routine while Sena slurped noodle soup. The small tourist community had changed attitudes and there were no raised eyebrows at my diet. Graeme dropped by with directions for Sena and we made our preparations for the little expedition.

I suggested that as it was customary to take a small gift when visiting a Cambodian home we shouldn't go empty handed. I was mindful of how bad I had felt in not giving Sek more. I was determined that I wasn't going to add another little torture to my collection. "So what should we take?" I said. Sena went straight to the cigarette counter and picked up a carton of 200 and then picked up a jar of sweets. "Surely we can do better than sweets and fags Sena!" "No really they'll like these." "Sure, but lets get something a bit more healthy." I picked up fish sauce "yes, yes get two bottles and salt and maybe oil. Get sugar too." I picked up some string and knives to go with it. We had quite a parcel. Sena explained to the shopkeeper what we were doing and she gave us a warm smile. We headed off to Krola Village, part of the Poey Commune in the hills above Ban Lung.

Even though I felt better that at least I understood why some of the burning was going on, I was sure that little of what I had seen so far fitted Graeme's description of swidden farming. It was the more likely pessimistic explanation of lawless land grabbing and logging. It had poor people tied up in the rich man's laws and had set the forest ablaze. Like the previous day there were plumes of smoke visible to the horizon and coming upon another fire that looked out of control yesterday's reassurance faded quickly. It was deeply disturbing. This wasn't swidden. The smoke and flames were so intense we had to stop and hope for the wind to change. I watched a couple of big trees virtually explode in the inferno. I remembered Graeme saying they didn't clear old trees so I was right to doubt. Sena talked to the solitary man watching the flames. "He says he's worried that the rains are coming and he won't be able to burn more." Bring it on I thought.

As we swung into the village I saw what appeared to be two men tugging a semi inflated weather balloon from a bag made of old carpet held by a third man. I was still trying to connect the improbability of such a scene with what my eyes were registering when  Sena said, "look they've just killed a buffalo." A puff of steam from the bag clarified what I was seeing. "Oh yes."

Sena made an enquiry and we were directed further down the village.

33 Low Tar

The village was set out in a neat circle with small rattan homes on stilts around the perimeter and a large meeting house in the centre, next to that was a small fenced garden of bananas. Three or four big kapok trees provided it with shade and showered the ground with soft white down. Like the middle of the day in suburbia most of the homes were quiet; I guessed everybody was out working.

We were told the chief was in Ban Lung and his son was out. Sena handed over the bike and one of the villagers went off in search of somebody to receive us. While we waited I took in the atmosphere. Though the structures were unsophisticated this was an ordered society. There was no litter, nothing ramshackle. Villagers were curious of course but respectful and mannered. The son

of the Chief arrived on the back of the moto wearing a sarong and an NGO project t-shirt. We explained that we would like to visit the village's Spirit Forest and presented our offering. He graciously welcomed us and accepted our gifts.

Cok Seth had a wide pleasant face with kind open eyes and a gentle manner. He said he would show us the forest and that they would offer the spirits some of our kind gift. Small portions were allocated to the spirits and we set off down the path. We passed through forest that acted as a protective barrier for the village and into maybe a hectare of swidden crops. It was as Graeme described, planted amongst the stumps crops of vivid green plants. In another area there were small individual family plots lined up like an English town allotment. It was easy to see the process working. The village had four Spirit Forests; we were going to the largest.

It was difficult to say how large the forest was but the spirit tree we were to make the offering to had big presence. There was no mistaking it or its importance. It towered out of the dense and luscious green jungle. Easily the biggest it was wide and it had attitude. As we walked into its small clearing a gecko like the one that lived in the Muslim house in Tum Ring shouted out and a chorus of insects and birds joined in. It was an oasis.

Cok Seth walked around the tree and in a high pitch trill called the spirits. I wondered if they would come for us. As a couple of the village boys set about making the offering Seth continued to call whilst tending the area, making sure it seemed that all was tidy for the arrival of the spirits. On an altar of large leaves small piles of sugar, salt and sweets were carefully laid out at the base of the trunk. A packet full of cigarettes were individually spiked onto twigs to make incense and the offering began. Cok Seth chanted while rhythmically tapping the altar with a small twig as a ring of low tar that would have appalled the anti smoking lobby gently puffed away. The simple kitschness and good intent somehow made the scene more wonderful. In short, urgent and lilting verses the prayer rose and fell and with each round Seth's concentration intensified. Sena beamed at me as he joined the rhythm clearly happy that he'd got me this far. I was beaming too, aware of the fantastic magic that had brought me here. The magic of a moment that was rare and unrepeatable. The here and now, standing beneath a giant spirit tree in an ancient Cambodian forest. The prayer was reaching its crescendo. Cok Seth's voice was clear and strong as he looked to the crown of the mighty tree and concluded the ritual. He brought his hands together in prayer above his head and withdrew bowing low in respect to its spirit; a swirl of ciggy smoke in his wake. I was touched by the simplicity and reverence and taking Seth's lead I also bowed to show my appreciation for the tree and its unspoilt home.

With the tree spirit, 'Sen Long' in Krueng, appeased it was time for the boys to lighten up and spark up their ciggy rations too. There was some banter between Sena and Seth and in a fog of nicotine we toured the other big trees in the surrounding forest. I asked if it was OK to touch them first and gave a couple a big hug. I was aware that my attitude towards the trees and whatever energy or spirit that might reside there was very different to that of the people I had encountered in the forest. Their relationship with the spirits was fear based yet I couldn't believe anything this beautiful could be malevolent. As Seth showed us rare fruits and enthusiastically pointed at different trees and insects I thought what a buzz to be in this heaven. It was all out of a National Geo mag and somehow here I was. If I'd thought about it this was probably how I might have imagined an undisturbed spirit forest but I couldn't have imagined me in the picture. If there were no spirits today this was surely blessing enough.

The others were starting back but I stopped to savour a stolen moment of solitude. In a quiet second would anything show itself? All was as it was but it dawned on me that if I had already received my lesson from the Kauri then did I need to be told again? I looked up and in a shaft of light a butterfly danced and I smiled to myself.

Back in the village Sena set himself up like Santa and started to distribute our gifts to the villagers. I was happy that he did this, as I didn't want to be the 'white man bearing beads'. Though it went against my principles Sena's cigarettes and sweets were well received while I was content with the look of appreciation for the more ethical goods. What struck me was there was nothing grabby about the process. Even the kids were happy with a sweet each as an elder took charge of the remaining stash.

The buffalo sacrifice across the village was part of some kind of celebration. Cok Seth told us that it was a family party and to join the celebration it was the custom to take rice wine. It was a Kreung 'bring a bottle party' and to go empty-handed would be as just a no-no here as in England. They asked if I would buy a bottle so that we could all go. I agreed and a guy went off on the moto. Sena cautioned that it would make me ill but didn't advise me to avoid it. More like shit happens but you've got no choice. I asked why. "Well they put the rice in a big jar and put rice husks on top and then seal it with mud. Then they leave it to rot (I presumed ferment). This is ok but the water they put in it probably comes from a puddle or something." The boy returned with a large earthenware jar and proceeded to break out the mud stopper and husk packing. Water from a couple of large gourds was poured in and allowed to settle. Then a hollow stick with a bit of rubber hose was rammed down into the base of the vessel. It was ready to drink. As guest and provider I was offered the first pre-party livener; I said a small prayer and took a suck. It had a kick but I could see the appeal. A nice warm afterglow followed the first harsh alcoholic hit. With everybody satisfied they'd had a good slug, more water was poured on top. Apparently more is added till it doesn't kick anymore. Nice idea I thought.

The party was cranking up across the way. Outside the house a shrine had been made from stout bamboo in an inverted pyramid to hold the head of the buffalo. Its last moments recorded in wide-open eyes and rolled back lip. Long lengths of rattan sprang from the centre of the structure, which hung low with woven decorations. It held me in a macabre fascination. Beneath the shrine a small family group ate with their heads sheltered by a cloth. Their hands moved quickly and they looked around furtively; there was an animalistic nature about their actions that frightened me. In a low structure in the yard the buffalo carcass was being butchered. A small group of men were chopping away at the meat transforming it into mince. The blood was driving the village dogs mad and vicious fights started over scraps. It was turning into a vegetarian's nightmare.

A line of ceremonial gongs strung from a beam was readied and then in time to the rhythm of the chopping knives they were played in a deep hypnotic harmony. Chung chung chung - Chung chung chung, the harmonics vibrated in my head and disturbed me. A man with entrails wrapped on a stick pushed passed and grinned a toothless grin. It was 'Apocalypse Now' stuff and I'd had enough. I was a voyeur on something I didn't understand and it felt wrong to be there.

I may have been projecting my own dark thoughts of blood, alcohol and ritual onto the scene but I was relieved though when Sena asked if I wanted to leave. Calmed by this decision I stopped to look around and in the moment it was clear that everyone was celebrating a rare occasion too – eating meat.

Our hosts cheerfully invited us to stay but Sena gestured to me and then to the sky and we mounted up and rode out to enthusiastic waves. Sena said as we left, "I told them that it was going to be dark soon and that you get frightened on the moto at night." I didn't mind sounding like a wimp. "I didn't think you'd want to eat the meat either. They might have been offended if you said no." "Thanks Sena, good thinking. Hey and we have our own party to go to"

As we buzzed along I reflected on the day. I was grateful for the insight I'd had as we left the spirit tree. I didn't need another 'experience' to cement in my mind the wisdom of the Kauri. It was always there. To search for a stronger 'hit' was missing the point. It was consumerism. The irony was clear as cold water. It was the cue to move on and do whatever I could with the new journey that was evolving.

34 Oiled

Back at the room I quizzed Sena on the logistics of finding the felled tree or tracking its brothers and sisters. "Do you think you might be able to find out where the tree went?" "I told you, it probably went to Vietnam." "I know, but what's the likelihood of tracking it down?" He was unsure; because of the ban the loggers had changed their tactics. "The loggers have got cleverer, like they get permits for transporting firewood. Maybe they don't use the main road like they used to. There are lots of places to cross the border too." I wondered if I found the tree whether I could somehow cross with it. It was upping the anti on the element of risk and I wasn't sure if I had the bottle. "If we found the tree this side of the border could I cross with it?" "That would be possible but the authorities are tougher in Vietnam if you got caught and I wouldn't be there to get you out either." Then he added more weight to the scales, "You know there's trouble on the border at the moment too?" "No, what's happening?" "Hill tribe people are coming over as refugees and the Vietnamese are angry." He explained that the Hmong tribe who helped the Americans in the war had been badly treated by the Vietnamese for their collusion and now they were taking their land. "The Americans have just started accepting some refugees and it's making the Vietnamese jumpy. I don't think a white face straying over the border without papers would be a good thing right now." My undercover cross border incursion had slipped away and I was thankful that I wouldn't have to test my heroism for now. "OK. What about we go up to the border and you can ask some questions on the way?" I suggested. "Sure we can do that. I know the Chief at the border." He said that if we took beer we could sweet talk our way right up to Vietnam. The guards patrolled a wide strip along the border and it would be impossible to get to the actual frontier without a bit of subterfuge. " I think they don't like people seeing what goes on up there." I wondered at Sena's connections, "How do you know the border guards?" "Oh, I come through here sometimes and I take beer and bullshit them! So shall we eat and then we can go to the party?" "Why not."

Josh and Hannah have a lovely old house and out on the balcony a dozen or so friends were drinking and chatting. Their holiday had started so everyone was relaxed and jovial. Graeme was laid back on a couch and I thanked him first for a fantastic introduction. Sena told him about the party and the rice wine. "I'm sorry I knew that it would be like that, it's why I made an excuse not to go. There's no way I would have been able to leave. I'd still be there and probably unconscious by now. How's your stomach?" "Actually, I feel fine." I'd forgotten I was supposed to be ill from the wine. Hannah introduced me to the others, Graeme chipped in something like the 'Spirit Tree Man', which seemed to be becoming my tag up here. Sena knew everyone.

Ian a Canadian guy seemed to take an instant dislike to me. It was as if he was continuing an argument he'd started with somebody else. "This spirit thing, it pisses me off. These people aren't Native Americans, don't project your desires for the Noble Savage onto them." "You know that's exactly what I realised today" I said. He stopped short, "I'm sorry, I'm glad you understand." "There's a lot I don't though." I added. After my ticking off from Graeme for taking photos at the Chunchiet Cemetery and then subsequently learning a great deal from him I was beginning to listen before voicing my opinions. We started again and realised we shared a passion for trees. It was clear to me that he could help me understand more. He had studied the Resin Trade in Cambodia and was now working with minorities in Laos to try and establish recognition for the trade there as a way of protecting the forest. From what he told me the situation in Laos seemed to be desperately close to the Cambodian experience a couple of years back. Since the logging ban hardened in Cambodia the trade had really kicked off there.

"In Attapeu Province, Southern Laos, just north of here, logging is really out of control. All along the Route 9 there are stockpiles of logs, stacked for miles." He said he'd recently visited ethnic Brao villages along the road that runs from Laos into Vietnam and had been shocked by the extent of the current logging trade. As the route crosses a few kilometres of Cambodian territory along the way I wondered to myself whether it would be a convenient spot to mix in some Cambodian logs too.

It really did sound like there was a frenzy going on across the border. "Logging was supposed to stop this year since so much was cut last year they actually couldn't haul it all. Only last year's logs were supposed to be transported to Vietnam." He'd stayed overnight in a Hill Tribe village close to the border and witnessed the extent of the trade. He said that all night, every 10 or 15 minutes, logging trucks had driven through kicking up the dust and making village life miserable. They were overloaded with massive logs and these weren't last year's logs, but fresh cut. He was bitter and angry, "So much for not cutting any new trees this year. The Villagers told me the trucks had been keeping them awake all night for weeks already." Ian explained there was nothing the villagers could do to stop the flow of logs as the army ensures there's no interference but ironically they're the ones being blamed for destroying the forests through their swidden agriculture. "The logging companies are causing the real damage. The ethnic minorities are just convenient scapegoats for forest destruction." Hearing the 'scapegoat' tag again I was beginning to see why people like Graeme and Ian were so defensive. They had taken on the challenge of fighting the weight of misinformation ranged at indigenous people. It was an uphill battle but they were both driven.

It seemed the trade followed the line of least resistance to Laos and without much consideration I said, "I guess at least we have to be thankful that the concession logging has been stopped here." I meant to sound positive but I just sounded naïve and insensitive. Ian jumped straight on my remark. "I wouldn't be too quick to say that. It's more like a temporary suspension; the large concessions haven't left the country remember." It was true the Cambodian government had announced logging and export bans in recent history and then all of sudden it was all on again.

I told Ian about Sek and the plight of the resin tappers and about how the sight of the rubber plantation clearance had shaken me. "Oh man, the whole plantation thing is obscene. In Laos they're tearing down the forest and planting Eucalyptus and Acacia for the MDF board industry. You know that Eucalyptus poisons the soil? Nothing can grow once they've planted that stuff. It's that whole idea that plantation timber is ecologically sound; they plant one tree for every one cut down. Well that's after they've destroyed the forest that once stood there and thrown everybody and every thing that called it home from people to wildlife into the road. There's nothing sound in spraying it with herbicide so that nothing grows between the neat rows of monoculture. Don't believe the label, don't buy it." I had facilitated Ian's rant it seemed but I was happy to have heard him. It felt like comradeship.

"So you guys ready for some more North Sea Oil?" Hannah brought in a tray with her Norwegian favourite, Schnapps and liquorice liqueur. "Or if you don't fancy that then you can try a Tequila Slammer." Inevitably the more foolhardy of us did both. "Here's to this guy." I said cheering Sena. He got a toast all round. "And here's to your Journey with the tree, Ken." said Sena, cheering me back. "What's this?" said Ian. "Oh, we came across a tree that had just been cut down. Sena reckons it could have gone to Vietnam though it may still be this side of the border. I want to try and find it and follow it to see where it goes. Maybe make some noise. I'm not sure yet." "It's probably on its way to being mixed up with Lao timber and soon to be garden furniture." "You reckon?" "It could well be, its big business in Vietnam."

I looked around to see that people were getting ready to leave. "We've been a bit boring as guests haven't we? Thanks for the info though." "Hey no problem. Let me scribble down a few book titles you should read." With that Ian headed off. "One for the road?" Said Josh. "Why not?" A final shot of alcohol was really more than we needed but we were within wobbling distance of our beds. There's a joy in walking under a starry night pissed and happy.

35 Green Rat Stew

The road to Vietnam was dusty and bare. For the moment the plan was no plan except to ride to the border; the chances of finding my tree were slim I knew. The people we asked in town said there had been no big log trucks through. I hoped that the intuition that made me want to stop the other day would lead me to something.

Inexplicably Sena had traded the trail bike for a step through. "This kind of bike is much better for rough roads." Odd logic I thought but he knew best. At least it was a late model and the suspension worked. A long hill out of Ban Lung was a test of Sena's riding skill and his choice of bike. The road had been widened but as the surface had degraded into deeper sand vehicles had pushed the boundaries in an attempt to find traction. A wide red brown strip of no man's land divided two thin lines of up and down traffic. The rains that would save the forest from more burning would make this a nightmare. I was guilty for my gratitude to the dust.

Small stands of forest remained but agribusiness had taken a firm hold. One estate had cleared four thousand hectares to plant palm oil, that's forty square kilometres of forest converted to a single monoculture. I tried to imagine how many creatures had died in the process. We stopped at another farm and Sena explained that three different crops had been tried there. Originally the forest had been cleared and Vietnamese workers had been imported to grow coffee. When this failed they grubbed up that crop and planted banana, which in turn failed, and cashews were planted. It looked a mess. To add insult to injury on the outskirts of Bor Kheo there was a sign proclaiming the office of the Forest Police. Three uniformed officers sat yawning on the veranda with nothing to police.

As we rode into Bor Kheo itself there were all sorts of preparations going on for Khmer New Year that would ring in at six o'clock that night. We stopped for a drink, Sena's favourite way to ask questions. "I say to people that the road is bad. It's a good way for them to complain about logging trucks breaking the road." There was nothing to go on though. As we were riding out though Sena pointed out a truck, "look it's got Vietnamese plates, that's what to look for."

By late morning we reached the border post 'The Battalion of Provincial Police 625'. This is the HQ of the guard that patrols a ten-kilometre wide strip along the frontier with Vietnam up to Laos and down as far as Mondulkiri; we had to get past here to make it to the door with Vietnam. It was a hot and dusty parade ground with some low tin-roofed barracks. Sena asked if we could see the Chief but he was out. His deputy was called. It looked like they had already signed off for the holiday as the deputy came to meet us in a casual shirt over his fatigues. Sena greeted him like an old friend.

Deputy had the look of someone desperately trying to remember on what occasion he'd made the acquaintance. He was a man of manners though and rather than commit a social faux pas he invited us in. A table was pulled out and we sat on the veranda under the tin roof and tea was served. Sena's performance was large; he was not going to let me down or let Deputy off the hook. Deputy had the look of a man trapped in a spoof TV show. He was waiting for the cameraman to dive out and say, "Hah you believed these were the Chief's friends but they are the infidel!" He was wavering. Sena grabbed Deputy's hand and placed it onto his knee; he put his arm around his shoulder. I thought this isn't going to work but Sena looked to me with a toothpaste ad smile "Can we buy these boys a case of beer?" "Sure." I said. Sena had him pinned down like a virgin in the grasp of a Bangkok Taxi Girl. The only way out for Deputy now was an ugly scene or submission. He gave in and the tension fell away but Sena kept Deputy's hand firmly placed on his knee for the moment. He said through Sena, "You must think we are not very disciplined drinking beer during the day." "No, no it's nearly the holiday after all." A few more of the ranks turned up and we were invited to stay for lunch and to help drink the beer.

A young guy appeared with the drinks. He wore a gold shiny

shirt with flouncy sleeves in the Saturday Night Fever mould. I thought he must be from the little store across the road but he was one of the guards dressing down for the day. He minced back in a trice with lunch. It was some kind of stew as green as new mown grass. I produced my bananas and French bread. Sena explained that I was a monk. But it's ok for him to drink beer? The Deputy gestured pointing to the glass and then me. Sena nodded yes. "Sena, what's in the stew?" "I don't know it has small bones like some kind of rat." Mmm nice I thought. "I have to eat it though." With everybody's glasses filled we stood to toast each other. It looked like being a session but it was good to be in the shade as the midday sun was intense and Sena was more than entertaining.

With more than half a case of beer already tucked away Deputy said he had something to show us. He reappeared from his office with a dangerous looking bottle of hooch. He explained that this was very special rice wine and invited us to try it. He poured a small glass each as carefully as if it were nitro glycerine. They looked expectantly on the monk. I popped it away with no problem, it was indeed good stuff. This met with general approval and they downed theirs. I thought I might gain a little extra kudos by doing it again and offered my glass for a refill. Deputy held the bottle close to his bosom and spirited it off to the safety of his office.

With a few beers inside him Sena was getting a touch overconfident and talked to me in theatrical whispers of how he had bullshitted the chief at this very checkpoint last year. I reminded him that he still had a moto to ride lest he got anymore cocky. We stood for yet another toast, it seemed the boys couldn't drink sitting down.

Sena went off in the direction of a pee leaving me with the guys. In faltering English the Deputy enquired, "So, how do you like Cambodia?" "You speak English!" Fuck I thought. "A very little." He said. I wanted to ask just how much of the following do you understand? 'Chief's friend, Bullshit, get them drunk, let the liars through,' but I said, "That's very clever of you," imagining a night in their slammer. "Ah, Sena the Deputy speaks English, isn't that fantastic!" Without missing a beat Sena said, "Shall we speak in English so my friend can join in?" To our relief it went over his head. Sena continued the conversation in Khmer, it seemed Deputy had rehearsed his question to me then didn't know where to go with it. I asked Sena if there was any word on log traffic. "Nothing they want to talk about. I used my road question ploy, they just complained that the new Governor paid one hundred and fifty thousand dollars for his job and he's making them work hard collecting bribes to pay for it. They say the road has got bad but he's not putting anything into repairs." "OK, have we done enough to go through?" "Sure, I'll tell them we have to go."

Like the magician's lovely assistant the boy in the gold satin waved us through with a low sweep as if we were to enter a wonderland. I wish.

36 Pant Boys

Beyond the barrier the road was rough but the movement restrictions encouraged me to think that the forest that started the other side would remain intact. Just over the first hill we came across the first of swathes of forest being burnt and cleared. We stopped to look. I got my camera out but Sena said, "No pictures Ken, we're being watched." "I don't see anyone." "Take my word for it."

Sena had a plan, "Listen I know where there's a log storage area the Viet side of the border. There's a village North of here on the Cambodian side that's easier to get to by crossing into Vietnam and back again. It's the route the locals use and the border guards let them go through; I'll try and get us across by saying we're going  there. Shall we try?" "Why not!" At the frontier guardhouse a stern official brushed Sena's charm aside with a wave of his hand. He tried again but he got a sharp mouthful for his persistence. "They won't let a foreigner through, I'm sorry." "Its OK, you tried."

We turned back but after just a kilometre or so Sena swung down a track; I wondered if it was his turn to follow his intuition. We headed into some degraded forest for ten minutes before stopping. "If we carry on down this track we'll probably be in Vietnam in ten minutes. Do you want to keep going?" "Sure."

We came to a bend in the Yali River, the destruction here was the more horrible because of the view to the other side of the water. Majestic stands of forest down to the water suggesting what a beautiful and intimate stretch this had been before. At the end of the track we came upon a small community living by the bank. We'd seen nothing that pointed to the progress of my tree; today was not going to be a breakthrough.

We sat on some rocks and watched children playing in the water and young women washing clothes. "Fancy a dip?" I said and we made our way down to the river. It was gorgeous. We sloshed about in the cool water with small fishes nibbling at our legs and feet. I sucked in as much of this moment as I could; it had the 'last day of the holiday' feel about it.

Sitting on the bank Sena lit a cigarette and puffed out a few contemplative clouds, I envied the habit for an instant. "So Ken, you know my family would like to have me home for the week-end. Do you think you can do anymore here, you know with finding your tree?" "I have a strong feeling I should go to Vietnam, maybe its already there." I said. "But you won't risk crossing here will you." "No, I'll go back to Phnom Penh with you and go the long way round from Ho Chi Minh up to the Central Highlands. Do you think I'm crazy?" "Sure but why not!" Getting up he said, "Its New Year at six o'clock do you want to see if we can get to the lake at Yeak Lom by then." "Sounds great." I emptied my bag of sweets for the children and we cracked on.

I waved as we went back past the post. We droned up the hill away from the border and through Oy A Dao, once a village surrounded by dense forest thick enough to hide the young Saloth Sar a.k.a. Pol Pot and his revolutionary guards at the height of the Vietnam war. Sena pointed to a small stream, "this used to be a river but since they cut the forest the rains don't come. No trees no rain they say." Up ahead a figure was struggling with an overturned bike. We found a lady scrabbling about trying to gather up the fish and blocks of ice that had spilled over the road. The bungies that held the cold box on and just about everything else together had snapped. She was unconcerned with the gash on her leg and worked rapidly to get everything back in the box. She got back on and gestured to wedge it between her legs and the frame. We heaved it on. She looked up from beneath her conical hat and gave us a thin smile. Despite the fact that she'd had quite a spill she flew off at top speed. "She was Vietnamese." "She looked scared." I said. "Probably of getting caught for a fat bribe." We were back on the road in a minute but on the next straight bit of road she was already half a kilometre ahead. "Look at her go!" I said.

We buzzed along past fields of cash crops. There was the occasional Cotton Wood or Chom Bak; the former considered worthless and the latter too dangerous to cut. It was the end of the day and the road was busy with people walking and riding home. Honda's thrashed past us, confident of the road. Cycles wobbled three up and minority people with their traditional cone shaped wicker backpacks strolled along in small groups.

Hanging out from the side of the road ahead were honeycombs on sticks; a guy seemed to be trying to catch punters like flies on sticky paper. Sena pulled up. They were natural forest honeycombs the size of large round baps. The forest bees that I'd found so trusting and that had been robbed of their offspring still buzzed around. My love of honey was seriously in question. "Do you like honey?" "I think so." We carefully put two in a bag; their attendant bees came along too.

We got to the lake before sundown. It's an ancient volcano surrounded by forest and filled with sparkling water. It was beautiful but we were back among tourists and purpose made swimwear. But what the heck, we did it in our pants.

Footnote. I discovered that only taking wild honeycombs results in the death of the brood. Beekeepers balance the needs of the brood with honey production.

37 Grub N Grab

"I've found you one without the little babies." "What?" I woke up to find Sena at the end of my bed with a piece of honeycomb dripping honey. Last night I'd watched him eat both of the one's he'd brought by the road. He'd broken me off a piece to try but as he did it revealed the tiny grubs inside. It was strange that I hadn't considered it before. I licked the honey off my fingers, which though beautifully fragrant was incredibly sweet and I marvelled at Sena's ability to polish off two combs in one sitting. "Thanks Sena but it's a bit early." "You're not going to eat it are you." He looked momentarily hurt and then gobbled it down. "I checked the flights. The pilots are working and there's one this morning. I'm going to get us tickets. I got a call too from Graeme, he's got some books for you, I said we'd have breakfast."

The first day of the Khmer New Year had brought with it rain. Outside it was fresh and the road in front of the hotel a deep red. While Sena biked up to the airstrip I walked across the road to meet Graeme for breakfast. No one was around so I sat down to watch the street. I heard a repeated thwack and girlish screams and got up to investigate. A guy was  whacking something with a pole about eight feet long while his girl hung back squealing. Clearly he considered it dangerous enough to need that kind of distance. He flicked something into the road and I went over to see that it was a beautiful vivid green snake. It twitched and writhed a few times and then expired. I didn't know, it could have been incredibly poisonous but I wondered whether it was killed just because it was a snake, a blanket of prejudice hiding its beauty.

Graeme pulled up on his motorbike. He sat down and gave me one of his intense enquiring looks then smiled brightly and said, "I have some booklets about our work with the Kreung village you went to, I thought you might be interested in reading them. I reckon the more people know what's happening here the better." It was becoming my defining purpose but I just said, "Definitely." "I'm sorry but I can't stay for breakfast but if you're interested I'll give you a quick overview. It might help with this tree trip of yours. What are you going to do now?" "I'm pretty sure I'll go to Vietnam and work my way up to just the other side of the border from here." "OK, then you definitely want to go to Pleiku, it's the first stop for logs from Ratanakiri it's also part of 'Triangle Development Plan." It was a scheme that the government was hawking about, he explained, to create an industrial agricultural area from Ban Lung to Pleiku in Vietnam, up to Pakse in Laos; hundreds of square miles of agribusiness. "It will mean cultural genocide for the indigenous people anywhere within the scheme."

The plan was completely incompatible with protecting the beauty of the region, the forest or tribal cultures but there's money in it for the vested interests. "It's already stimulating land grabbing and the Prime Minister is adding fuel to the frenzy by saying 'Go to Ratanakiri there's land there. '" I had read articles about new legislation but as I asked the question I just sounded naïve once more, "but what about the laws that protect Indigenous peoples' land." "There's no law here Ken. It's probably hard to imagine but there isn't any public service." He stopped for a moment; he really did mean me to imagine a place without law. "Nobody really works for the government or the people because everyone pays for their job from the governor down; public service becomes private service, people are just looking for a return on their investment." It was sinking in as he went on. "There'll be no forest security till there's land security and what's happening here will continue while donors believe that development is good for local people." Now he was questioning another basic belief, "Surely it does some good?" I said. Graeme nodded a 'nope'. "One of the ministers was up here saying what a great thing the new airport would be. He was after good headlines in Phnom Penh, talking to the press about bringing prosperity to local people. I asked him what good would it bring indigenous people? They don't speak Khmer so there won't be any jobs for them." It was a simple observation that would easily be lost in the news coverage but was a fundamental flaw in the plan. That's if they really had in mind helping poor people. He pointed out that the development would suck in more people from outside to build it and run it, which in turn would fuel more land grabbing, destroying what's left of the forest. "If they cared about local people they wouldn't have allowed a hotel to be built on a sacred burial ground. It's just about creating opportunities for opportunists; what's happening here is comparable to what happened to Australia's indigenous people, they're destroying the communities." "A Cambodian 'Rabbit Proof Fence'," I offered. "Exactly."

"Ya Kuak, the Krola Village Chief said, Indigenous people need land and forest, not money. The forest is our market." He smiled, his sharp enquiring smile and sensing that I'd grasped what he had to convey said, "I've got to go, say goodbye to Sena for me. Good luck with finding your tree but if you don't you know you're bound to find something else." "I already did, thanks for everything and thanks for all that you're doing too." Graeme smiled, stuffed his helmet on and buzzed off down the road. Sena missing him by minutes came back with confirmation that we were on the flight. We grabbed breakfast and checked out.

We waited for the incoming flight while tourists and NGO workers assembled in the little wooden terminal. A European guy carried a crossbow and other ethnic souvenirs while an affluent Khmer family had a parrot in a cage, tokens from a disappearing world.

38 Chamau

As we settled into the flight I flicked through the information Graeme had given me. I opened one of the photocopied and plastic bound documents at random. An account by a villager from Krola jumped out. It was of the 'forest people', creatures that live between the boundaries of the spirit world and earthly existence. The indigenous people of Ratanakiri call them the Chamau.

Some tribes describe them as little white people with blonde hair who are responsible for mysterious laughter and gong playing in the forests but this version was of something altogether scarier. "It has one leg and hops. It has the head of a person but the face of a dog. Its hands are knives, and it's leg is like a dog's leg. They have long hair past their waist and eat the tips of rattan and coconut. We used to see it but not so recently. It doesn't kill people but it's cruel. It chases people screaming. I was chased by one during the Pol Pot time." The footnote said that indigenous people had given an early explorer Capt. Baudesson accounts of a similar creature during his travels across S.E. Asia; which had a razor sharp membrane on its forearm to slice through branches and undergrowth.

The book was part of an examination of spiritual beliefs and practices put together in response to the threat of the Hero Taiwan Company logging concession that still hangs over the area, and which includes Krola Village. The concession to log out the area would be a disaster for indigenous people like the Krueng. For them everything has a spirit or 'Arak', the forests, trees, water and their swidden gardens, the 'chamkar.' The most powerful and foreboding is the mountain spirit, the Arak Chendu. Daily life for them is a spiritual one; the spirits are everywhere and must be respected. They believe there are dire consequences for any form of insult.

It's a belief system that has done much to protect the environment and to prevent conflict with other tribes. There are strong taboos that regulate their use of the forest resources and which maintain their boundaries with others. It isn't the appealing Native American Indian view of nature; a higher understanding of our connectedness with everything rather the spirits are like stern elders or policemen.

The Arak Chendu, the mountain spirit, the strongest can act together with or even in place of the other spirits. The article went on; for example if someone angers the Arak Nam, the house spirit it might be Arak Chendu that meters out the punishment. "If we don't respect the house spirit, it can send us to the Arak Chendu," explained a villager. "The house spirit is like the head of the village, while the mountain spirit acts like the policeman. If someone does something wrong in the village, the house spirit can complain to the mountain spirit who will take action." The outcome for even irritating the spirits can be a swift and severe punishment according to the locals. An account of such retribution struck home, particularly as I was at that moment some ten thousand feet above the forest below and possibly swirling in the vapour of its Arak.

It read, 'The village of Krola has a spirit forest called Prey Arak Thom (Large Tranuk). (The Tranuk is a rare type of tree and Cok Seth had showed me its fruit). During the 1970s when the government was building a road through the region, construction workers disrespectfully slept under the spirit tree for the night. Three people died the next morning and two more died when they arrived back in Ban Lung.'

It was fascinating reading but in the circumstances a tad disturbing. I decided to save it for another time. I entrusted my safety to the god of small aircraft and made a mental offering to the spirit of the bald tyre.

PILGRIMS PROGRESS

Heading to Vietnam is like the prospect of Christmas with the in-laws. Theoretically it should be a great time but there are unspoken rules and conditions on the invite. I was not bearing gifts and like the old blues ditty though my intentions were good I was sure to be mis-understood.

39 Freedom Trail

I had less than two weeks to get up to the Central Highlands of Vietnam and back to Phnom Penh if I was to make my pre-booked flight back to England and a rendezvous with Bunty. On the way back from the Airport I went straight to the Vietnamese embassy and got a visa then booked a bus to Ho Chi Minh City allowing myself a day to rest. I had plenty to read up on; a report by Global Witness which Mike gave me called 'Made in Vietnam, Cut in Cambodia' about the garden furniture business suddenly looked particularly relevant. It was written at the peak of the industrial logging epidemic in 1999 and documented a logging

route from Ratanakiri to Pleiku. I didn't have a guide but the information it contained on the routes, furniture factories and people involved at that time would be a good start. Pleiku was in my guidebook as a backwater destination. I could try for the border from there and check out the furniture factories for any evidence of Cambodian timber. After that I'd go with what came up.

I spent my day off getting my clothes clean, checking my mail and running all the things I'd seen and done round my brain. Sena came by and I paid him up for his great job. "It's not about the money you know." "I know that Sena." I said pressing the money in his hand. "You've been fantastic and I really appreciate you giving up your holiday. Please thank your wife for me." "Let's have a beer at my house when you get back from Vietnam." "Sure. Oh and I'd say buy yourself a new knife but I don't approve of that kind of thing" He bashed his head with the flat of his hand. He'd forgotten all about it. I booked my regular moto boy for a six thirty a.m. pick up and crashed in front of a DVD, 'Apocalypse Now' seemed appropriate after where I'd just been.

The coach to Ho Chi Minh City (HCMC) pulled away on the dot. I should have remembered from my last trip to Vietnam the 'to the minute punctuality' of their busses. I just had time to stash my bag and grab my seat. It was full of western tourists and I noticed the look of dismay on my neighbour's face as I sat down. He'd clearly thought he had a double seat for the trip. Big seats for small minds I thought.

We edged out of Phnom Penh through the sprawling slummy suburbs and then joined Route One our road all the way to Vietnam. It was a couple of hours of brown fields till we got to the Neak Loung Ferry across the Mekong. It was famous for a serious bombing by the USAF and it still looked a mess. Not far from the crossing we stopped for breakfast. I sat with a Philippine Christian Missionary. She spoke excellent American English and I was intrigued as to what she was going to do in Vietnam. I came to the conclusion that she was going to 'worry', about the water, the food, the people and the religion. I explained that there was a large Roman Catholic community in HCMC but it was clear that wasn't her brand of Christianity. She seemed as worried about the R.C. as she was by the Communist government. I decided to leave well alone.

It was hot enough to melt the tar on the road, if there'd been any, as we arrived at the border crossing. The bus emptied and a couple of porters loaded the bags onto a trolley I presumed was going to our bus on the Vietnamese side. As they scurried off I thought 'that was silly to let them take my bag, I'm travelling light'. We lined up to exit trying to find shade anyway we could. With no revenue to be made from punters leaving the country by land very little is done to make this process quick or convenient and we waited for best part of an hour while one official watched by two others thumped a rubber stamp over a busload of passports.

By the time I got my exit stamp I was beginning to get worried about my bag. I hadn't seen it since it got wheeled away by the two doubtful looking characters an hour earlier. I found it and them standing in no man's land. They had provided no useful service and were trying to extort a dollar a bag. A couple of Western ladies in front of me had already given in to their aggressive 'no dollar no bag' routine. I grabbed mine from the trolley and took great pleasure in telling them to shove it. I tried to help my countrywomen retrieve their packs too but they didn't want any nastiness. 'Good afternoon Vietnam,' I said to myself.

Across the border we became 'consumer units' in the Vietnamese Tourist Machine. It's ironic that in a Communist system capitalist entrepreneurs, maybe unwittingly, have created perfectly the reality of western life; the illusion that you are free to do whatever you like, in comfort and safety. The majority of visitors will travel what has become known as the Sinh Café Trail. It's a coach route from HCMC up the entire length of the coast to Hanoi. Travellers buy an 'open ticket' that's good for the whole journey or sections of the route and stop off wherever they like along the way. It feels like complete freedom to roam until you want to stop anywhere outside the published stops or stay in a guesthouse other than the ones they take you to. Buck the system and try and do it your own way and it gets difficult. It can feel like you're under surveillance the moment you step off the coach, for instance when I was in the country before I dipped out of a provided breakfast to experience the street food and was pursued by the coach boy to find out why. So unless you're ready for a struggle they'll take you where they have it sewn up and you'll see what they show you. It's an example of how well we've been conditioned in the west that some don't even seem to notice they're being controlled.

Predictably as we pulled into HCMC or Saigon, as even the locals seem to prefer, we stopped outside the Sinh Café in the backpacker area of Pham Hgu Lao. The approved accommodation reps had already been on the bus to hand out their details. So when the doors opened to a pleasant welcome from their counterparts ahead of the clamouring hoard of accommodation gatecrashers, it was obvious who would get the travellers' business.

With a light bag I was quickly away though I wasn't out to prove anything, except that I didn't need to waste time going through the room run. I found a nice enough little place and went out to see if I could get a bus up to the Central Highlands, maybe even that night.

Most of the tourists if they are venturing away from the coastal route will head for Dalat, described as the 'Jewel of the Highlands' I was headed for the more work a day Pleiku a good deal further north. I was too late for that evening's night bus but booked for the following night. I had a night and day to enjoy Saigon.

40 Billy No Mates

Millions died trying to hold the Capitalist line in Vietnam and yet here is one of the most entrepreneurial races on the earth. If the Western governments had realised that this would be the outcome of a unified Vietnam it's hard to imagine they'd have fought so hard. Surely they'd have waited till Uncle Ho popped off and got down to business as usual.

Once I'd left attachments to comparatively laid back Cambodia behind and moved up a gear I remembered I liked Saigon. There's still plenty of French style architecture to enjoy and a depth of culture that recognises its worth and refuses to lie down. I love the way that families will create a homely space on the pavement in the evening. They come out to watch the street like we retire to watch TV. Mother will be cooking up something tasty on a small grill while dad sits in his vest talking to the kids or passers-by. By eleven thirty all will have gone to their bed and the pavement becomes a pedestrian thoroughfare again. Imagine how much safer we'd feel in British city centres if families dragged out their living room every evening to commune with their neighbours; how sheepish the drunken teenagers would be at chucking-out time with real people to watch them rather than anonymous cameras.

Food is everywhere, catering to the Vietnamese need to eat every twenty minutes it seems. If it's not on the street it's in the street; from vendors to little roadside restaurants set up as night falls to serve delicious food; collections of child-size dining sets clustered around a cloud of cooking steam. I even found one of my favourites Com Chay, which roughly translates into Vegetables and Rice except the vegetables are textured and flavoured to look like meat. Crispy duck and other traditional dishes made from soya and who knows what else are served up in the Vietnamese way so I didn't feel left out.

Killing time before my bus I wandered around town. If it weren't for the terrible traffic it would be a delight. It was on a previous visit I learnt to cross the road Saigon style and it has stood me in good stead but nevertheless it still takes some balls to walk slowly out into a wall of traffic and accept that it will miss you. The central market, Ben Thanh resembles the one in Phnom Penh built in the Art Deco style though in much better condition. It's packed with goodies and a selection of food stalls for the ever-peckish locals. Saigon is a shoppers dream but I was ...hing I picked up here. I decided ...the homeward journey.

...ur office to my bus waiting out ...ably only a hundred yards away ...ey make sure you don't stray. I ...ou always get a number and I ...ing companions. I was the only

...he low sun shining through the ...ed up the voiceless kareoke to ...f for a fourteen-hour trip. The ...atered agriculture of fruit and ...rkness filled the window lines ...plantation rubber trees flashed past in their uniformity; straight rows stretching into a dark infinity.

Late in evening we stopped at a coach stop and everyone piled off. Though I'd filled up with food before we left I was getting a Vietnamese snack attack. The fare looked very meaty and the ladies working the big saucepans looked blank at my Com Chay? I ordered tea and munched through a packet of biscuits while reading my book. A smart looking guy walked up to me and kindly asked me my name, I told him. "And where are your friends?" I said that I didn't have any I was travelling alone. He looked slightly distressed on my behalf and appeared to be looking round the restaurant for a little friend for me. I tried to make him understand that I wasn't without friends just that I didn't have any with me right now but he continued to look worried, "This is really very sad that you don't have any friends. I'm so sorry but my bus is leaving now. Good luck." He walked and then turned clearly sharing his concern about my lonely state with a couple of his friends. They waved and boarded their bus.

Our driver had finished his dinner and we were boarding again, I squeaked out a last pee in the mosquito-infested toilet and jumped on. It was time to settle down for the night and blankets were brought round. Thankfully the kareoke was switched off and the lights dimmed but the seat width was narrow and the recline shallow. My neighbour, a young girl, rolled up a jacket and made a pillow on the window, I resigned not to get any sleep. Sometime later I woke up to find that the girl had nestled into my shoulder and my head rested on hers. I woke her to apologise and to establish a respectable arrangement. She returned to the head-bumping window and I to a decent English bolt upright. The next time I woke in the same predicament I accepted that this was actually comfortable, gave in and slept.

The sun was up when the bus made a pee stop. It might well have been that Vietnam was one huge rubber plantation because as I looked out the window on the sunny morning we were in another one. It stretched into the distance, one huge monoculture. Pleiku is a working town and the roads were busy with people going to work by bus, bike and step through. There were few cars to choke the wide roads. The coach stopped outside the hotel I'd pulled out of the guidebook just long enough for me to grab my bag out of the hold before grinding a gear and leaving me in a plume of diesel.

The choice of rooms in the hotel was between modest priced grim and stupid priced not so grim. Wiped out as I was I opted for the 'not so grim' white concrete cell in which a colour-blind acidhead had been allowed to go mad with the soft furnishings. There was a telly with umpteen fuzzy Vietnamese channels and beneath its lurid cover the mattress was marshmallow with walnuts. The toilet had a reassuring ring of paper over the seat, which proclaimed it had been cleansed but by the look of it with a coarse grade of sand paper and road dust. Despite the fact there was an ashtray on every surface there were long cigarette burns on everything including the cleansed seat. It was as if they'd got the habit of burning ciggy's for incense too. But hey it wasn't a bumping bus. It would have been easy to try and sleep for another few hours but with so little time I had to make every day count. I went into town to find a guide.

41 No FSC in VN

I was on my own now. I was aware that I was running on empty emotionally and physically and I felt vulnerable. I had to keep focused. I ran the plan through my mind as I walked into town. The different strands were coming together now. I should travel the route of my tree as best I could. This is what I sensed the tree spirits had instructed; the purpose would be revealed I was sure. The most logical route from the border would come through here and on to the port of Qui Nhon. If my tree or the brothers and sisters were consumed by the furniture industry then there's a good chance that Pleiku was part of that route.

At the tourist office I found a small team waiting to serve. It looked like they'd been waiting for sometime. It brought back the feeling I had as a small child entering the waxwork museum of Madame Tussauds. Waxy fixed grins. And then they came to life; it nearly made me jump. I enquired about buses. "Why do you want to go to the border?" said the man at the desk. He had a waxy suit and waxy comb-over hair. A small shower of dandruff had settled on his shoulders like dust on the surface of an old record. I had only vaguely prepared a story; I hadn't thought I'd need it yet. "I'm travelling in the footsteps of a monk who walked from Burma to the South China Sea. His route would have taken him across Vietnam from Ratanakiri in Cambodia to the sea at Qui Nhon." "I'm afraid that you cannot go to the border." "Why is that? I have come such a long way and it would be bad for my spiritual quest if I cannot go there and tread the footsteps of the holy man." I said larging it up. "I'm really sorry the military would stop you. They will not let anyone pass." "Why?" "I'm sorry I don't know." I went to sit down and think. They brought me tea and gave me their folder of organised tours. Waxy comb-over came to sit with me, "Maybe I can show you some of the other fascinating things here?" I tried the pleading game once more, "You know I have travelled many hundreds of miles so that I can walk this path." "I'm so sorry but you know it is only thirty-five kilometres, that's not much more than twenty miles. Maybe you don't have to travel that little bit." I flicked through the book.

I would need to travel that bit if I was to be completely true to the notion of a pilgrimage but how important were those twenty miles? I may never know but now was a time to be decisive. I decided to move quickly to my objective in Pleiku. Maybe I'd get another chance for the border later but for now, just keep moving I thought.

"I'm also interested in visiting furniture factories." I said trying to sound as nonchalant as was possible switching from the spiritual to the commercial. "You want to go shopping we have many interesting shops for you to look at; furniture, art and ethnic articles." "No I would like to go to a factory that makes garden furniture. I have a garden design business in England and I'm looking for a supplier for many pieces." He tipped his head to one side and stroked his chin. I thought he's clocked me, but he said "OK, I have a friend who has a factory, I will call him to see if he can see you. When would you like to go?" "Now would be good." "Please wait I will try." While I waited I thought I must get my story together, I didn't sound very plausible. The Global Witness report named names and I wondered how sensitive they might be to outsiders asking questions around here. "OK we can go to the factory, you would like more tea first?" A big breakfast would have been the go but I could deal with my empty stomach later I thought. My guide introduced himself as Hai, despite the awful comb-over and nasty suit he was easy to like, he was bright and friendly and spoke very clear English. The driver Thieu had a sharp angular face with a scar on his cheek and a thin moustache. He could easily have been a 'B' Movie baddie.

As we arrived at the Duc Long Furniture Factory I fretted that I looked more like a traveller than an International Buyer but I had little choice. The gentlemen in the office wore cool western chinos and white shirts; I looked exactly like I'd been crushed on an overnight bus from Saigon. Hai made the introductions and acted as interpreter. The company director asked me what I was interested in. I told him that I had a garden design business and wanted to expand into furniture sales. He sized me up but no more than I'd expect in any commercial meeting; he wanted to establish how many container loads I was worth that's all.

I described my customers as a mixture of commercial and residential consumers. I asked about shipping and timescales and asked if they were able to interpret the computerised drawings of my own designs. I sounded plausible but he hadn't seen the colour of my money yet. He asked if I would like a tour of the factory and showroom. I was introduced to the production manager who took me off in the direction of a large complex of factory buildings. I asked to see the whole process.

I guess I had somehow expected a cottage industry so it was a big shock to see acres of production. It looked like something from the big days of British manufacturing complete with streams of overalled workers. I steeled myself for the logical start of the tour, the stockyard. Round logs were stacked ready for the mill and it was whining its way through the giants. Clearly the Production Manager didn't see this part of the process as anything that would interest me and gave the area a cursory introduction and was already moving on. I was fixed to the spot. There they were laid out like corpses, wonders of the forest reduced to commodity. I started to crumble; the walls were falling in a wave of depression. I was losing it. The manager brought me back with a call to keep up. My project was in the balance. I pushed up one more barrier and rejoined the tour.

"After the timber is machined it is boiled." We stood and watched a worker skimming off the resin from the boiling water. I worked at getting a grip. I found a part of me from another time in my life when the forest was not a concern. A time when profit margins were things I seriously considered, a time when it would be easy to connect with the motivations of the people here, people making a living. A detachment was forming over the raw feelings like dead skin. I can do this I thought. "This will remove the resin and then it is dried in kilns." He said. "What moisture content remains after seasoning?" I'd found the question from the literature but it had an authoritive voice. "Oh about eight to ten percent."

We went into the first part of the production line. Small teams of workers carried out repetitive tasks to a roar of small power tools in an atmosphere of suspended dust. The Production Manager shouted that including their facility in Saigon they had over a thousand workers. This production hall led to a finishing facility where ladies with hand-held sanding machines took off the edges. Away from these units the finished furniture was dressed with oil and finally packed into customer branded boxes. I asked where the finished products were heading. He explained boxes with logo's 'The Living Table Company' were going to the UK and 'Garden Impressions' to Holland though presumably for the UK or US market because they were printed in English. "Where does the timber come from?" I asked "From Laos, Malaysia, some from Vietnam. Last month my boss brought 3,000 cubic metres from Malaysia but our customers don't like it. It cracks too easily and they say it's not as hard." I bit my lip and let the comment on the 'returns policy' for trashed rainforest go. I couldn't let a comment like that trip me up. Before we walked back he showed me the expanding facilities; an automated line about to come on stream, this was all brand new with overhead rails for efficient movement of pieces. "Soon we will start using this system for more production."

Back at the office Hai and the director talked in Vietnamese and I imagined it was to find out more about me and what kind of deal I was good for. I looked at the glossy company brochure. The picture on the cover showed the head offices standing in a beautiful forest. "Where is this office?" I asked, breaking up their huddle. "It's here." Said Hai, gesturing to the facility, "they superimposed the forest on the photo." "Virtual forest." I said, Hai nodded and laughed. I flicked through the catalogue using cues to ask questions. "So how much furniture do you produce?" "From here we ship thirty to forty large containers every fifteen days." "So what can you pack in a container?" "Oh, probably one hundred and fifty of these sets." The director pointed to a garden table, parasol and a set of four chairs. I tried to do the mental arithmetic but it wasn't happening with all the stuff going off in my head. I tapped out 80 x 150 and got 12000 on the desk calculator, I had to do it twice to be sure I wasn't going over the top. "Wow twelve thousand table and chair sets a month, that's good business." The director looked pleased at my recognition of the scale of his achievement. "I see that you have expansion plans." "Yes, we have already doubled in size this year." "So you're buying your timber from Laos and Malaysia?" "Yes and we use Vietnamese plantation rubber too."

I was ready to ask the questions I'd wanted to ask since I'd arrived. "So do you use any Cambodian timber?" "No, nothing from Cambodia." I changed track, "My clients only want to buy environmentally sound products. What safeguards to you have in place to make sure that what you use is sustainable?" "Everything is FSC certified, so you know it's sustainable. See it's here in our brochure" I could feel myself going red, 'the fucking liar' I said in my head but kept cool. "But that can't be. Laos and Vietnam have no FSC accredited forests and there are only three small ones in the whole of Malaysia." Now he wasn't sure, I'd set off alarm bells and definitely pissed him off. "No, everything is sustainable." He was closing the books and closing our meeting. He was avoiding eye contact too, "Perhaps you should decide what you want to buy. Then we can talk some more." He didn't mean it of course but he didn't know if I was trouble. I hoped I could be. "Of course, I will be in touch." I said, somehow wanting it to seem like a threat. It was over and Hai walked me out to the car. I let out a shout inside my head.

Note:

The Forest Stewardship Council [FSC] is an independent international organisation which provides an international standard for sustainably harvested timber. The FSC brings together groups such as timber traders, indigenous peoples' organisations and environmental groups.

Timber companies who want to produce or sell timber and timber products to FSC standards undertake to follow strict harvesting guidelines and undergo independent verification from the concession to the end user. The FSC logo is the nearest thing to a guarantee that the timber concerned really does originate from sustainable sources.

42 Love and MDF

Back in the car Hai asked if I'd seen what I wanted. In reality I'd rather of not seen the extent of the trade. In fact I'd rather that I'd stayed on the beach and not got involved. It would be easier to believe the convenient lies and the green tick logo in the brochure that said all was fine and that I didn't need to worry about a thing. At that moment I wanted ignorance but the truth was out there now. I still had the pretence to keep up though and mindful that I'd paid him for half a day out of a dwindling budget I asked if there were any other factories to see. He explained that he would need to go back to the office to try and make arrangements with other companies; that we could go out again this afternoon. I said I'd think about it. We drove back to town in silence, Hai tried to initiate a conversation but I was stuck with the thoughts of the scale of the business I'd just seen. I could tell he was keen to hang onto the possibility of more work from me this afternoon. There wasn't much else going on. "I know where you can see more furniture on the way back. Do you want to go there?" It seemed pulled out of nowhere but I thought why not. It was as I suspected a waste of time; we pulled up by a small roadside furniture shop. There was nothing but nasty examples of cheap veneered wardrobes and laminated flatpack. The sweet family who ran the place dusted off a chair and I sat down hungry and despondent. Hai joined me to talk "You know I have a small garden I was wondering if you have advise." Bless him I thought, "Not without seeing." I said. "Maybe if you have time." "Sure." "Do you like this kind of furniture?" He pointed to a white laminated computer station that would fall apart with little more than a thump. "It's not really my cup of tea." I said. "Its very popular here because its cheap. It's made of MDF board." I thought about the conversation I'd had with Ian in Ratanakiri about MDF. Then there was the email that I'd regularly received asking for my name on a petition against plans to turn a huge area of the Amazon Rainforest into woodchip. Though that campaign was won I wondered whether it was possible to use tropical hardwood like my tree in MDF? I tossed in a chance remark, "I'm interested in that too." "Really? You know we have the biggest MDF plant in Vietnam here in Gialai Province. In fact I think it's the only one in the country." Without thinking the plot through I said, "Can you get me an appointment to see it?" "You wish to visit the factory?" Said Hai with a bit more than surprise. I could see why. This morning I was a pilgrim with an interest in furniture, which had now been stretched to Medium Density Fibre Board production. "Why do you want to go there?" Without a story I thought that no story was the best way so I asked again. "Can you get me an appointment?" "I will try. I will come to the hotel later and tell you. If not can I show you some other sights?" I thought I'd galvanise his efforts towards getting me an appointment. "No Hai, if I can't see the factory then I will catch the bus to Qui Nhon."

I was so hungry I was ready to gnaw my fingers off. We arranged to meet at the hotel later and I went off in search of food. The guidebook recommended a place popular with westerners, though I was yet to see one and went off to fill my belly. I found the restaurant but as I got to the door the owner waved me away. It was closed. I walked along the small strip of 'Com' rice stalls but they were finished or just had gristly bits of meat in cabinets. I went into the market to see if I could find anything there. There was the bus station café with a few steaming saucepans but the diners, a group of rabid looking men jeered and laughed as I approached. I felt like a twenty-three stone stripper at a truck drivers Christmas party. The chances were it was steaming offal anyway so I didn't bother. On the corner there was a French bread sandwich stall. If they had some Laughing Cow cheese I'd be happy as Larry. My 'Pho Mai?' for cheese met with a blank. I'd probably used the wrong intonation and asked for dog breath or something. I brought bread and then got some bananas. I was on that one again. I shuffled back to the hotel and decided to sleep off the frustration and anger like a bad hangover.

The phone rang but in my sleepy clumsiness I pulled it from the wires that came straight out of the wall. By the time I'd swore and twisted the connections back together who ever was there had gone and there was a knock on the door. Hai was waiting in the lobby. "Are you alright?" I obviously looked like I was degenerating. "Yes, I just woke up and I broke the phone." He looked puzzled but this was going nowhere. I asked about the appointment. "Yes the director will see you. Tomorrow is his day off but he will see you." I congratulated him, he was clearly happy that he'd pulled it off. "So tomorrow we go at eight o'clock?" "That sounds great. I think from there you can take me to Qui Nhon." "Oh yes, that would be a good idea because then I can make an excursion for you." He was happy that now it would be a full day trip.

"Hai, I'm very hungry and I can't find anywhere suitable for a vegetarian. Can you help?" "I was thinking you don't look very well. I will explain to the lady here what to cook for you. Do you like noodle?" "Yes" "Do you eat cheese?" "Yes" I nodded like a donkey with Parkinson's "Do you eat egg?" "Yes" "And vegetables?" "Yes!" "OK then I tell her to make noodles in the Vietnamese way but with Vegetable stock and tomato soup with cheese." I could hardly talk for salivating. "She will go to the market now and cook everything for you. Can you give her a little money?" "Of course." "Then I will see you tomorrow."

The hotel had a small western style restaurant bar that looked pristine almost certainly because no one ever used it. It was more than likely too expensive for locals and few Westerners stayed here. It was surely opened with high hopes of big dollars but its Pizza chain furniture had seen few bums on seats. Tonight for me it was the Savoy. I nearly wept as the kindly lady laid out the table with her best doilies and fussed about with a candle lamp. A large cold beer was poured and out came my feast. The love and pride mingled with the fantastic aroma. I did my best to repay her by eating slowly till the very last scrap. We were both so happy.

43 Heavens Above

I looked out the window to see the silver Mercedes was waiting.
B movie baddie was having a big nicotine hit. I watched for a
moment the way he sucked on the cigarette. There was nothing
contemplative about it as he rushed to get it all down, one big
suck followed by another. Just breathing like that would make me
dizzy. I went down to have breakfast and check out. I asked the
lady how much my dinner was. She gave me what was clearly
a local's price, which I couldn't accept after her beautiful meal.
I paid her what it meant to me and made sure that she knew
how much I'd enjoyed it again. She disappeared blushing and
thanking me. She re-emerged with her little daughter and the
bellboy and they stood round me bowing, thanking and grinning.
Somewhere from inside a great ball of emotion came rushing up,
all the held back grief was rolling over itself in a wave that was
about to hit. I bowed and 'wai'd to them before rushing out.

Thankfully Hai had not arrived and Thieu had started another
cigarette. I sat in the car getting a grip. Once all the emotional
stuff was back in the boxes I thought about my story for the
director of the MDF factory. I had no idea how I was going to
explain my interest in his works.

Hai arrived bright and cheerful, "Good morning. Did you enjoy
your food?" "Very much Hai, it was all that I hoped it would be."
"Ah this is good because I cook these dishes myself so I explained
to her just how to cook it." "So I hope you have enjoyed our
town also." "Of course. I would have liked to stay and see more
but I have a tight schedule." "I am very angry with the Lonely
Planet book you know. They don't say very good things about
Pleiku. Do you think you could write and tell them how much
you enjoyed it here?" "Perhaps I will." We drove out of town and
onto the main road to Qui Nhon. I wondered whether I'd left my
tree behind or if I'd find its spirit by the sea.

"It was a shame I couldn't get to the border." I said. "I'm sorry
too. I wanted to take an American ex-serviceman there recently

to a hill he fought on during the war but they wouldn't let me go." "So why?" "Oh you know it's very primitive there and I think also there may still be bombs. I'm sure they will make everything OK there soon." "I heard that maybe there was trouble with the Hill Tribe people, perhaps that's the reason." "I don't know." Hai shrugged and looked out the window avoiding my gaze.

"So now we are on our way to the factory. It was very lucky." Hai paused and then looked at me with a little grin and raised eyebrow "I think I know what your purpose is." Shit. I pretended that either I didn't hear or understand. "So, how old were you when the war finished." I said moving on swiftly. As if he couldn't help himself Hai slipped straight into his regular job of taking war veterans about. "Oh I was about seven." Just to keep him on track I commented on the lack of vegetation. "Did they drop agent orange here?" "Oh yes and napalm." The scenery was quite dramatic though barren as we climbed into the hills. Thieu was driving like a getaway specialist. Hai was now established in his tour bus patter. "This is the Mang Yang Pass, it means Heavens Gate in the Jarai language. Pointing to an old outpost "and there's a tomb to the Unknown Soldier. This place was very dangerous for the Americans, there were many ambushes along this road. They dropped lots of defoliants here to destroy the jungle." We reached a plateau and I looked back on 'Heavens Gate'. It was true it looked like a gateway to the sky. "And here is an old battle ground where the French were defeated in 1954." "That's right I saw the fiftieth anniversary poster of the battle of Dien Bien Phu when I was in Saigon." "Yes that was the big battle in the North but there was fighting going on all over the country." I told Hai how I'd seen a documentary about Dien Bien Phu when I was a kid. How inspired I'd been by the Vietnamese spirit. The French had a major garrison there surrounded by a mountain range. They considered it an impenetrable fortress until Uncle Ho's army carried artillery pieces and ammunition up the side of the mountains on bicycles to fire down on them. They laid siege on the French for fifty-seven days. Ten thousand beleaguered soldiers surrendered defeated and shattered. "Those Viet Minh were so determined to fight for their country in the truest sense."

"That's what people didn't understand in the West about the American War. It wasn't about the North fighting the South. It was a peoples' war for freedom."

As we headed down from the hills into An Khe we passed villas that could have been Mediterranean, bright red bougainvillea covered the roof and terrace of one little home with its fence to the road. Kids with untidy bundles of some kind of crop flew down with us on bikes; there was a rural fifties South of France about it. After the French shipped out this town later became home to the US Calvary though by then they'd traded their horses for helicopters. Stationed here were 15,000 servicemen and four hundred choppers.

Then not far out of town were the smoke stacks of the Gia Lai MDF Factory. A yellow and blue complex surrounded by high walls and double metal gates. The Director came down the steps to meet us as we drove in. I still hadn't come up with a plausible story so I decided to gush at him. I strode forward and gave him the Enthusiastic English Buffer, Terribly Good Show treatment; I shook his hand vigorously and thanked him very much for seeing me. "What a marvellous factory you have." It did the trick. He spoke very good English. "Would you like a tour of the works?" "Oh yes please. Super." We viewed the raw materials being dumped into a feeder. "Here a mixture of Eucalyptus and Acacia is chipped and then hot washed." It was definitely Eucalyptus as the smell was very aromatic. I scanned around to see if I could see anything more substantial. I was looking for the tell tale pyramid of red logs, any sign that it wasn't what he said it was. There was a reserve of split wood ready to be chipped but that was all. We walked on. "Then here it is dried and blasted into fibres and mixed with resin and wax." He said pointing to a wide aluminium structure with fat piping going off in all directions. "Fantastic! Is this all new equipment?" "The factory is a year old but all this equipment is second hand. It came from Metsa a Finnish company." "And the factory runs seven days a week." "Yes seven days a week and twenty four hours a day." "Incredible." We went inside and stepped up a gantry to where a wide continuous sheet of brown fibre as fat as a mattress was extruded onto a conveyor belt. Eight foot of it rolled into a press as the cover came down slicing it off the strip. With a hiss of compressed air and a waft of heat the cover came up to reveal a neat sheet of MDF. The director turned with a satisfied look. "Bravo" I said.

From here we went into the control room where half a dozen technicians watched over the process on computer monitors. I gave the director a nod of admiration. Then finally we went to the end of the line where a forklift truck stacked all the finished boards onto pallets according to the thickness. There were probably fifteen people on the whole factory floor. "So how many people work here?" "We employ one hundred and fifty people, we operate three shifts over twenty four hours. Would you like tea now?" "Oh yes please." We went up to the offices, which had an Eastern European technology feel. I could imagine a Soyuz Space probe being commanded from such an environment. We queued to wash our hands in the directors' little hand washbasin then sat down for tea. I anticipated some questions from the director so I decided to get in first. "Thank you once again." I gushed. "Here is my card," he interrupted. "Oh I'm sorry but I've had so many meetings since I got here, that I've run out." I read his card. "Thank you once again Mr Pham Trong Minh." "That's OK." "Can I ask you about the output of the factory?" "Yes, daily we produce 180 cubic metres. Our output for the year is around 50,000 cubic metres." I scribbled down the figures in my notebook wondering if this would be suspicious. "And do you have plans for expansion?" "Oh yes, the market in Vietnam is probably for 200,000 cubic metres and we should grow our share by ten percent this year." "How do you guarantee your supply of timber?" "Through reforestation projects we have provided a one hundred percent sustainable supply." "You only use Eucalyptus and Acacia?" "Yes" "And you have published details of the reforestation project?" "Yes, you will find them on our website." The director stood and bowed slightly. "I think we have finished now." Clearly he'd decided he didn't think much of the Englishman. As we breezed down the hall he gestured to the administration department and then we were outside. We shook hands, I'd given up on the Basil Fawlty act now and we pulled out. Across the road though was a major pile of tropical hardwood behind a high wall with barbed wire. "Hai can we look at that company across the road." "You want to look at the logs. Of course." We crossed over to look but the view was better from the higher ground on the factory side. The gates were shut and a nasty looking dog salivated at the grill. "They make furniture here but today it's closed. I don't know why." "Where do the logs come from, do you know about that." "Oh they come from many places to Gialai. Laos, Cambodia, Malaysia and Myanmar, it's well known."

In contrast the MDF factory looked like a model and apart from the black smoke belching out of the stacks what was there to criticise? U.S. Military thinking that deemed an entire ecosystem expendable in a war over an economic system perhaps. The destruction of ancient forest that makes plantation seem like a healthy option?

44 Heavens Right Here

In the shade of the next stop on the itinerary I explained the theory I'd been developing over recent weeks to Hai. It seemed a good opportunity to try it out. "A little while ago I stood on the edge of a forest and washed in a beautiful stream. I thought at the time that this is heaven on earth, but what if this is heaven?" I said pointing to the earth beneath my feet. "That actually we are born into heaven. Think about it. We arrive in god's kingdom without the benefit of an introduction and an overview of the set-up by his right hand man; we just have to figure it out for ourselves. Perhaps it's the exercise he's set us? Instead of a joining pack of infinite wisdom to reflect upon we are born fresh and innocent into this heaven we call world.

It could be that we have a chance here in paradise for a greater understanding before we are born again on earth. After all why should we get eternal bliss just for avoiding the major pitfalls of life, for being nice?

Buddhists believe that once a soul reaches enlightenment it will cease to be reborn. When there is nothing more to learn the endless cycle of rebirth and death will cease. So in my thinking once the person attains their enlightenment here in heaven they will not need to be reborn on earth; the soul will spirit free in the ether of a higher energy.

If we knew that this is heaven, I've been wondering who would destroy the ultimate creation? Would we cut down its beautiful forest and kill its amazing creatures to try and create something more beautiful or deemed more useful. Would we kill another soul in heaven? Would we abuse a heavenly child?"

Hai and I had arrived at the first stop on his tour to find that it was shut for lunch. We walked around the gardens of the Quang Trung museum and stood beneath the central statue of Nguyen Hue. He'd been big in the Vietnamese history but he sounded like another warlord to me. I thought one thing we have to change is the way that being a complete bastard is a way of ensuring longevity in the memory of your subjects.

It was hot in the sun so we retired to a shady spot by an old laterite well. It turned out that this was Hai's hometown and as a kid he'd camped out here. He asked me about my religion. I told him that I didn't really have one but instead I got inspiration from lots of sources. He asked if I knew about Cao Dai? He explained that this sect had taken its inspiration from all the major religions, Christianity, Buddhism and Islam and created it's own in the 1920s. Cao Dai was the 'One Eye'.

We got talking about our beliefs. It was good to talk to Hai; he'd been brought up with communist anti religion so now he was experimenting with his own thoughts too. I'd been kicking around some ideas but the great thing about conversation is that once you have to explain your thinking it becomes clearer in the mind. I run the concept that this earth is actually heaven past him. He found flaws in the logic but I argued that surely there are plenty of holes in the established religions. Many get round this problem with the concept of faith, not to question but to believe. I asked him to consider anything that could be called god's creation and offer it up to my 'this is heaven' concept. To reinforce the point I picked up a frangipani bloom from the grass. The construction is a beautiful symmetry, the pure white petals tipped with yellow and the scent of, heaven. He liked it.

It was time for our lunch too and we stopped in town. A little roadside place was open and Hai ordered up some noodles in vegetable stock for me. It was served with bunches of herbs and freshly boiled eggs. "You know its nice not to be taking war veterans around," he said. "I bet. Do people harbour bad feelings towards the Americans?" "No, there's no animosity, people just say 'no war, we're happy." "That's great to hear." "No, I like the veterans but they are often very sad. They start to talk about their experiences and then they cry. They ask me to forgive them." "That sounds like hard work." "Yes, recently a veteran told me his story. He was a paratrooper and he said that he was dropped into an area near here. While he was coming down on his parachute he was very easy to shoot but the local militia didn't kill him.

When he landed he got his gun and shot the Vietnamese soldiers as he had been trained. He was very very sad and cried a lot for the bad thing he had done. He wanted me to forgive him." "Poor you and poor man to have carried that guilt for so long." I thought in the West he'd get training for the service he provides. It was a lovely lesson in letting go of hate.

Before I slipped completely into my counsellor-to-counsellor mode the sombre mood was broken by a lovely little boy who had been taught to say hello in English "How are yooo?" We all laughed as he ran back behind the curtain to re-emerge with another greeting of "How are yooo?" "I'm fine. How are you?" I replied. This routine would go on for as long as the adults had stamina to continue.

Hai looked at his watch and said that we really should be getting a move on as they didn't want to return to Pleiku in the dark and we still had a distance to travel to Qui Nhon. We drove on an old road built by the US through the Ruou Bau Da region. It's famous for its rice wine and Basaltic soil. Brick kilns line the road like the ones outside Phnom Penh but without a ready supply of rainforest timber to fire them they run on sawdust or coal. The Aon River offers irrigation to the paddies that in turn provide a splash of green to an otherwise dry and arid landscape. There's no forest here to bring rain. It's something that's initially hard to get used to, the absence of forest; we grew up with Nam movies, there was always jungle. Not now. I've been here for days and I've travelled a third of the length of the country and I've yet to see any forest or jungle.

An old Citroen 2CV came floating towards us as they do on two foot of suspension. Old ochre and faded blue buildings took me back to France again and then a riverside town and its colourful pagoda made me call for a photo opportunity. I'd hardly got the camera out since I got here so this was a great shot. Chinese iconography against a vivid paddy, a couple of farmers in conical hats; it was the perfect example of the view we have of Vietnam. My guide was clearly panicking about time so I snapped a few and then jumped back in the car. We sped past an 11th Century Cham Tower but clearly this was not on Hai's itinerary.

A narrow raised road crossed the Bay of Thi Nai, the shallow flat water provided a mirror surface for the brightly painted fishing boats. There was nowhere to stop for a photo here, it was one to commit to memory. On the other side of the bay we met the outskirts of Qui Nhon. It declared itself with the presence of boat builders, shipping containers and heavy vehicles parked besides the road.

As we approached the high walled and guarded port gates Hai asked Thieu to slow down, clearly he knew I'd be interested. "Can you see the logs there?" There was a large pile of round logs in a dockyard compound. "And there, the trucks loaded with logs?" We pulled up. "Be very careful how you watch here. If they see you with a camera it will be confiscated." "Sure, thanks for showing me." We carried on to the sea front and Thieu pulled up outside the guesthouse I'd selected from the book. I wished them well and waved good-bye. I wanted to see as much as I could before the sun went down.

45 Wing Ana Hope

If I'd been in the sandals of my fictitious monk I'd be at the end of my pilgrimage; the South China Sea was lapping in the bay. The task I'd taken on was by no means over; Qui Nhon was another waypoint on the Journey.

I decided to walk down by the beach to think. The fleet of colourful fishing boats anchored on the edge of the municipal beach would be a good place to start. I kicked off my shoes and walked down to the water. As I stood with my feet in the sea I looked back up the beach, a couple of fishermen scowled at me. They gestured for me to clear off. What I had taken for their squat down and chat was in fact a shit and chat. I was standing in the toilet. I gingerly made my way back up the beach through a minefield of turds.

With probably an hour of daylight left, I decided to walk back to the port and see if there was a better vantage point to see the logs in the compound or maybe even blag my way in. It was probable that my tree or its relatives passed through there, either as a log  or in pieces of finished furniture packed in a container bound for Europe or the USA.

I walked along the paved promenade to the end of the beach. In the shallow water there were 'Chinese' fishing nets and pulled up on the sand were the round coracle boats that I presumed transported the fishermen and their catch back to shore. It is a fishing method proven over hundreds of years. As a neat juxtaposition half-submerged into the sand an American tank stood testament to the redundancy of war as a solution to anything. I avoided the 'Siem Reap and Ratanakiri' Zoo in the street behind the beach. As the name implied its inmates were looted from Cambodia. I didn't need to add to my grief.

A high wall enclosed the port with warnings in English against tresspass and photography. I followed the perimeter in the hope of a break. A truck appallingly overloaded with huge round logs squirmed past me. I counted ten hulks piled on its back. I wondered how it didn't just collapse under the weight. I headed off quickly in the direction it had just come. Around the public quay a busy hubbub of commerce, banter and colour cheered me up. It led out onto a long jetty where more fishing boats were moored and rafted together. Some carried strings of powerful looking lights and would no doubt be heading out soon to deceive and capture fish with artificial suns above their nets. From here I could plainly see the log pile and decided to see if I could get to it, maybe I could touch and say farewell.

A waterside community appeared from where I stood to sit inside the port wall and so I decided investigate whether there was a way in from there. From the main road I dipped into small narrow lanes full of life and trade and followed my shocking sense of direction in the hope of connecting the location I'd seen from the Quay with the one on the ground. Any hope of discretion disappeared as I had acquired a following of excited children calling out and laughing behind me but I walked purposely onward. Beneath my feet concrete had given over to timber above water and apart from being hopelessly lost I'd strayed into a labyrinth of walkways that I sensed were not thoroughfares. Soon I was at a dead-end in somebody's living room. The family were understandably very pissed off that a stranger had just walked in unannounced with a dozen hysterical children. Harangued by grandma with the backing of the rest of the kin it looked ugly. I Wai'd and humbly apologised for fear of a lynching. I turned to leave quickly but I was trapped in the melee created by children pressing into the space and those bolting from the telling off. I tried to push through as granny worked herself up into a full on rant. A young girl with a bicycle seemed to add to the impossible logjam but she called out to granny and then to me in English, "follow me please." Her presence seemed to quiet the situation and with the giggling kids sent on their way she reversed her cycle out onto the paved path and directed me to follow. Soon we were back out on the main road. Though she looked about thirteen and a little too small for her bike she said she was twenty-one and studying for a degree in mathematics. "My name is Wing, what's yours?" I told her and thanked her for helping me. She nodded that it was OK. We had the usual conversation about age and marriage and children. She was very earnest about her study and hopes for the future. I couldn't help thinking that she was a product of a system that was so appalling to the West that millions were committed to an early death in an attempt to crush it. Her parents would have been 'gooks'. We came to the road I recognised as the one to the port head and said goodbye. She said "if you are going to the Internet later I'll see you there." She got on her bike and cycled off in her pristine white Ao Dai.

Approaching the dock gates rows of trucks waiting for their loads lined the road. This was where Hai had stopped beyond the entrance. I could see the logs from here but I was aware that to stand and look would attract attention. A line of trees and undergrowth behind the parked vehicles was clearly the trucker's toilet so I used taking a leak as an opportunity for getting a closer look. The logs all had a white number or marking on the cut face. I remembered that the logging companies mark their logs with an I.D. in white paint together with a metal tag that is supposed to identify the origin and logging company owner for timber in transit. It's a much abused system but it might make tracking my log possible if I could take the numbers and do some research. The light was too dim to take a picture with my long lens.

I walked towards the gate; it was guarded. A moto boy pulled up beside me and said, "you want go in?" Without another question I got on. As we pulled away he said, "You have permit?" "No" But he carried on the 50 yards or so and pulled up by the guard at the gate. The first of the lorries loaded with logs was only another 50 yards away. If I could get to them I could note the number plate of the truck and the ID on the logs. The guard pointed to the permit sign and gestured for mine. I pulled out my UK Driving licence and gave it to him. Clearly he couldn't read the English but the photo matched my face. He wavered. I willed him to be confused enough to let me through. I smiled my best smile till it hurt my cheeks. He flipped it over again, looked at the picture, and looked at me. He paused to consider then gave the card back and waved me away. I took a last look at the logs as the moto turned back out of the gate.

"Where you want go now?" Damn, I'd been close but maybe there'd be another opportunity "The Internet shop." I said, thinking that perhaps I'd have mail from Bunty or word from the Cambodian connections.

46 Mental Dadio

With my head down and my mind still on the logs in the dock I nearly walked straight into his bicycle. He looked like he'd just walked out of an asylum dressed in a white housecoat, a thick brown woolly hat and wearing a grin as wide as his ears. I apologised and went to pass but he had me trapped between his bike and a row of white teeth. He said "Woo yoo lark too come too myee parr goda?" like a slightly gormless Vietnamese relative of Janet Steet Porter; his voice was completely at odds with his handsome face. I could see that the Internet café was packed so I thought why not. "Where is your Pagoda?" "It ears farf kalom meters. I can take yoo on myee bi

cycle." I popped onto the flimsy rear carry rack, wedged my feet on the wheel nuts and we wobbled into the evening rush hour. Apart from roundabouts, which were particularly hairy, our sedate progress along the town streets brought a smile to my face. It was the perfect antidote to the stresses and upsets of the day. My new friend introduced himself as 'Minh The' and tried to make conversation from his position some way above me. I discouraged this as I couldn't understand his pidgin English over the noise of the traffic and every time he turned to talk he swerved dangerously. People stopped and stared at the Barang and the monk as we cycled along. It was another loony pilgrimage but this new project had me laughing by the time 'Minty' announced "This ears myee par goda."

The sun had set a long time ago and I could only just about

make out the entrance. Through the arch was a big old Bhodi tree and beneath it an ancient shrine with a sitting Buddha surrounded by candles. An old man prayed with lit incense. It was gorgeous. However, standing above and behind this atmospheric place was a new octagonal glass structure with fluorescent lighting, fans and plenty of kitsch. The Buddha was decorated with heaps of shiny material and surrounded by a halo of coloured lights. Minty showed me around and was clearly proud of this new blot on the landscape. I paid my respects to the Buddha and dropped some Dong in the donation box. I told Minty how beautiful the Buddha was though I knew I didn't actually mean this structure. He invited me for tea and to meet the other monks. There were just five. Minty had the best of the English so the conversations were short but you could have dried your washing on the warmth of their smiles. The mosquitoes on the other hand seemed to be more taking than giving and I was picking up a worrying collection of bites; Minty gave me a little jar of the local Tiger Balm, which smelt like floor polish. Though it seemed to keep them away the smell induced a slight feeling of unease associated with a new school term and a freshly polished assembly hall. Blimey the power of aroma I thought.

With the tea drunk and the available English consumed I said that I should head back. I thought I might just get a moto but Minty was insistent that he took me back. "Yoo come to myee par goda. I will take you back to town. Kenfinn I also tell yoo some fing. I fink that yoo are my men tall far th-er." I paused for a minute trying to piece his sentence together. "Ah. Minh The, I am happy to have you as my mental son!" Bless, I knew he had no hidden motives; there'd be no begging letter in the post. He grinned and pulled on his woolly hat for the return journey. I wondered afterwards whether actually an inch of close knit might not be a good thing in a spill.

I checked my email. There was a short message from Bunty. Her course was nearly finished and she was studying hard for her exams in less than a week. The time was running out on my excursion too and I had to decide how best to use it. I tried to be clear headed about what I could achieve now. After today I accepted that I would not find my tree in Vietnam, certainly not intact. I had reached the furthest waypoint, Qui Nhon and the sea. I would be returning to the journey soon enough; my flight to England would bring me back on track. Now there was a detour to take and I decided to concentrate on gathering information on illegal timber, the furniture trade and if at all possible witness something coming across the border.

I went back to my room to make a plan. It was tempting to stay on the easy coastal road and go back down to Saigon to look at furniture factories but I read more of the Global Witness report about the routes for timber out of Cambodia. Mike from GW told me that there was evidence of routes into Vietnam from Mondulkiri. Looking at the map there was a good excuse to get close to the border with Cambodia in the Yok Don National Park about a hundred kilometres South West. There's a thirteenth Century Cham tower at Ya Liao, right by the frontier. I thought maybe if I got there I might be able to trek around the forest and see if anything was occurring. I would have to get to Buon Ma Thout and find a guide and get a permit according to the guidebook but it seemed like it could be done. I asked the guest house if they could arrange a coach down the coast a bit and then I could cut back into the Central Highlands by local bus but this proved to be unworkable and the only option was to backtrack to Pleiku and down from there. It also meant a five a.m. start. I would have to be up for four-thirty but in the end I had no need to worry about over sleeping. An intermittent stream of trucks thundered by and every now and then I felt compelled to get up and see if that one was loaded with my tree.

47 Hole in the Wall

The hotel boy had written down my destination on a piece of paper and arranged a moto to pick me up. I was just pulling away when he ran out with my passport. We laughed but I resolved not to leave it with a guesthouse manager again.

The town was bigger than I had imagined and as we rode out to the bus station I watched the early morning regime of exercise that seemed to have gripped the town like a scene from a futuristic Kung-Foo movie. It was five-thirty a.m. but down on the promenade men and women in regimented ranks of white tunics practised Martial Arts with wooden staffs. Out on the main road joggers of all ages ran in packs of ten to fifteen, by the University the jogging broke into running. Athletic young men and women sprinted along the campus roads. It was if a siren had gone off somewhere and families mindlessly left their houses in their pyjamas to obey their leader. Once they were ready he would send them out to kill, like Ninja automatons.

The bus station was new with a flash glass temple terminal in the middle of a square of pristine tarmac. There wasn't a clapped out bus to be seen just rows of late model Mercedes and Japanese mini buses. I was actually hopeful that this would mean that the tourist friendly Sing Café mentality had made it here. I asked for buses to Buon Ma Thout. I was obviously the twenty-three stone stripper again as a bus full laughed at me. It was obviously too early for me, on another day I would have been able to shrug them off; even out do them on banter but this morning I was fresh out of humour.

I asked the guy with the bus and the cardboard sign for Buon Ma Thout how much? "One hundred and twenty-five thousand." "That's eight dollars!" I said. The bus was full and ready to go but shit I wasn't paying eight dollars. I went and sat at the coffee stall outside the gate to think. Touts surrounded me; word was out that someone had asked the Barang one hundred and twenty-five. Though he'd walked away he was bound to cough up in the end, after all where was he to go? The sad logic was dawning on me too. Eight dollars was worth it to be on my way even if it was well over the top.

As I walked back along the buses the touts moved with me like the small fish that clean the mites off sharks. I found another bus bound for Buon Ma Thout and asked how much, "One hundred and fifty thousand." Now it was ten dollars. A polite man came to my rescue and gestured to the glass temple terminal, he walked me to the ticket desk. Of course I thought, I'd get an official ticket at the proper price there. I showed the girl my destination written on the piece of paper. The girl looked to the man; it was now clear he was a tout. He wrote a hundred and fifty thousand on the back, she was of course going to charge whatever he said. After a small protest I handed it over. I was allotted my seat and I sat down to wait for the bus to fill. I stewed in my anger. A lady selling the usual selection of useless plastic items and sweets came to the open door. She smiled a winning smile. I could be a miserable old git for the day or I could let it go. I bought some peanut brittle sticky enough to pull out my expensive dentistry and gave in. I watched the locals while we waited.

If half the population exercised obsessively, the other half smoked for Vietnam. My travelling companions were outside getting the nicotine down before we set off, sucking like baby lambs on teats. They'd put beagles out of business in the West. With nearly all the seats filled we were away. As a token of value we were given scented towels in plastic like the ones you get in Indian restaurants heated in the microwave. As we were travelling in a late model Mercedes mini bus with aircon it seemed a waste so I popped it in my bag for later use, perhaps on a Cambodian bus where it would make sense.

The conductor seemed redundant in a 12 seater but he made up for it by hanging his head out the window like a slobbering dog calling out our destination in an incomprehensible slur. By the time we cleared the town the spare seats were filled and he sat back to distract the driver who'd obviously been to the same 'getaway driver' school as Thieu.

It was the road I'd travelled the previous day so I ticked off the landmarks in reverse. Up on the plateau we stopped for breakfast. In a small concrete blockhouse a couple of ladies were cooking up something that was clearly off my menu but by the door another was making pork and salad French stick sandwiches. I managed to make her understand that I didn't want one with meat so she simply dragged out the floppy slices of pork from one she'd just done. I was too hungry to be picky about it not being strictly vegetarian and woofed it down. The salad came with sea-flavoured sheets of crispy dried snot, which actually tasted great. We stopped briefly at the top of Pleiku before heading on. The scenery while not stunning was at least green as it flashed past but there was no jungle.

The bus pulled into the station situated that infuriating three kilometres from town thing. It's a very popular arrangement with moto drivers as it ensures there's always a fare to be had from an incoming bus. In Laos it's possible to travel miles by bus on fifty cents but then the moto boys will try and get a dollar for the few extra into town. The only consolation for being ripped off on my fare here was that the trip into the centre would seem good value. All the same I made the bastards work for it by getting my pack on and feigning that I was going to walk. I took pleasure in whipping them up into a frenzy. They rode round me like Indians circling the wagon train but I broke for a small space in the perimeter wall. Seeing that I was going to get away a moto sprinted to get to the gap but I got there first and thumbed my nose at him. It was a great laugh. Out on the road I found a nice old boy with a clapped out moto who clearly needed the fare more than the hustlers inside.

'Vietnam the Destination for the New Millennium' read the sign over the tourist information office. The door was shut and our hosts for the new destination were stretched out asleep on benches inside. I knocked but nobody was coming to open up. It was twelve-forty and the office shut at twelve-thirty till two-thirty for lunch. I hoped it wasn't the two hours that screwed my chances of getting to the National Park in a day.

I needed to draw some money and get something to eat so I walked into town. A stream of restaurant hustlers ran out with their menus to entice me in but one after another offered only pork noodles or pork grilled. Even the market had pretty much packed in for the day, just some sad trodden vegetables and live catfish in bowls left out in the sun. I wanted out of here.

To be fair on Buon Ma Thout it's actually quite a pretty little town but with hardly any sleep, a bus rip-off and an empty stomach I didn't need much else to go wrong. I went to the bank, which the guidebook said did credit card encashment. The counters were empty. A solitary girl mimed that the bank was closed for lunch. I showed her my plastic card and asked if they did encashment. She shook her head but I didn't know whether that was no or I don't know. I blundered out into town hungry and broke. I was too pissed off to enjoy the fact that the Vietnamese leave their doors open when they go out to lunch, even at the bank. I walked into the street of restaurant touts but turned quickly lest I strangle someone. It was all going tits up.

I decided to wait for the bank to re-open, at least it was air-conditioned inside. The girl behind the counter came out with a glass of water, bless her. She even showed me to their cloakroom where I rinsed my face and cooled down. At two o'clock the clerks returned to their desks and I asked about getting cash on my card. They looked blank. I sat down despondent. The guard came over and tried to help. He was pointing in a general direction but I'd already walked that street. I asked him to write it down but in Vietnamese I didn't understand the script. A lady who looked like the manager came over; she had better English and tried to explain. I asked them to point to the street on the map but no one seemed able to comprehend the concept. She sat down next to me as if to consul me and said "my bank does credit card encashment." "Please tell me where your bank is." I said in desperation. "This is my bank." I showed her my card "You can give me cash?" "Yes follow me." We went to her office and she swiped my card. Nothing. She swiped it again. Nothing. She called for a technician. He wiggled the wires and checked the paper roll and swiped my card. Nothing. I imagined a huge bill building up back in England. An hour later and probably twenty swipes later she gave in. I walked out as broke as before.

Back at the tourist office they were up and awake. I asked about getting to the park and hiring a guide. They had no guides. "What about calling the one mentioned in my guidebook?" I suggested. "Yes it would be possible." "No, I'm asking you to call him for me." "Ah, of course." While we waited he told me of his study of the English language. He had cultured his Jeeves accent for sure. The man from the book was there in five minutes. I told him I wanted to go to the Cham Tower by the border. "No. It's not possible. I went with a Japanese tourist last week and the soldiers turned me away." "But that was last week." I said. "No it will be the same." I asked why but he shrugged his shoulders. "Is there a night bus to Da Lat?" "No all buses are gone, why not stay here and go on an excursion with me tomorrow." said the guide. I asked, "How long it would take to get to Lak Lake?" It was about half way on the road to Da Lat. "About two hours by moto." "Can you take me now?" He didn't want to go so tossed in a high one "Ten dollars!" Screw it I thought why not? "OK, but we have to find a bank, I need to get cash on my credit card." "You don't need a bank. Look there's an ATM across the road."

48 Mr Nasty

Somehow it was good to be on the back of a scrappy old moto out on the road again, it felt free. Though it was costing me dear at least I was directing the show. We pottered along with the rural evening rush hour through an agricultural countryside. It was pleasant but unremarkable. The road slowly climbed into a range of hills that eventually looked down onto the valley below. There were scraps of forest but the landscape had taken some serious knocks. It was not hard to imagine how beautiful the view from this trail must have been but the land had been badly looted. It seemed what was left was being busily loaded onto trucks: sand, rock and timber. We passed through villages that once would have been tucked away from the world inside the jungle but now they were just dust stained and fly blown.

At the top we looked down on a greener view. Below us Lak Lake and its lowland paddies offered a more promising prospect. We coasted down and stopped at an ethnic village by the lake, it was geared up to extract tourist dollars with rows of trinket stalls. My guide explained that there were tribal long houses overlooking the water where it was possible to stay for five a night. The light was fading so it seemed like a good idea to establish somewhere to stay right away. A stunning young lady in western clothing greeted me from outside the ethnic information hut and confirmed there was accommodation available. She asked me to follow climbing the notched log in her stack-heeled shoes up to the long house veranda. Inside was forty foot by ten of empty floor space, I had somehow imagined staying with a family or at least sharing it with other travellers but I was the only guest this evening. She pulled out a mattress and plonked it down. It would seem strange sleeping in such a large space but I imagined the view in the morning would be fantastic so I said it would be fine. She gave me the padlock key and I waved the moto away.

She asked for my passport. I'd decided that I wasn't going to part company with it again after this morning and besides there seemed very little security here. This morning had been a wake up call so I told her that I would be keeping it. I explained that I would write down all the information she needed in her book but I would keep it. She insisted but I politely declined. She asked me to unlock the door, and then told me to get my things and go. Chucked out onto the lane my options looked slim. "You want scarf, hammock?" A lady in one of the gift stalls called out. I asked about somewhere to stay. "I have menu, why you not eat here and then my son will take you to the village to find somewhere?" It seemed like the best offer all day so I sat and drank a beer while her daughter practiced her English. There was enough food for two but I seemed to develop a secondary stomach it was so good. I asked about buses to Da Lat. She told me that there were four, every half an hour from six till seven thirty in the morning. I planned to be on one however nice the view of the lake was. Her son took me to a concrete guesthouse in the village. It looked like they had just cleared the punters from a wedding party, as the place had been devastated. In the back room a few diehards were strangling a kareoke. The room they showed me was featureless but I was too tired to be concerned with charm. I just wanted to sleep and be on the six o'clock bus.

We went back down to register. They wanted my passport. I explained that they could take the details down but I would be keeping it. They insisted too and told me that I would get it back in the morning. I watched her fill out my details then asked for it back. "No, we will keep it. You will have your passport back at seven thirty." Ah, I twigged. They keep your passport till all the buses have left then you pay some extortion for a taxi. I already had the key to my room. "Here is the five dollars for the room and I'll take this." I said tossing the money and snatching my passport. While they argued between themselves presumably over who should have been watching the Barang I scurried up to my room and bolted the door. Minutes later they knocked but I called out that I was in the bathroom and to go away. They shouted and banged some more before giving up. I had a full belly and a litre of water, I wasn't coming out.

I broke out my cosy up rations, a small pack of incense, a

candle and the peanut brittle. I had my personal stereo to chill to and soon I could reflect on things in a different mood. I got to thinking about the extremes of the day, the kindness and the rip-offs. I wondered about my heaven on earth theory. Perhaps this is hell too. Would that fill some of the holes in the proposition? Would a loving god create perpetual suffering as the price of failure, what would be the point? I don't see extreme vengeance as an aspect of any god I can conceive. Higher teachings are of love, tolerance and forgiveness. Would all that go out the window the moment you cark it and arrive at the pearly gates? I don't think so. No, it would make sense that heaven and hell co-exist here as they do on Earth. God has created a place so beautiful it can inspire the qualities he wants us to aspire to. This heaven is full of the things we need to sustain our bodies and to lift our spirits. It's for heaven born babies like you and me to find our goodness and to shine the light on ignorance. Now I just wonder how Earth will be. Maybe it will be better when we've learnt how look after heaven.

I was stirring as the six o'clock bus tooted in the street; I was out the door by twenty past. Last night's moto boy was waiting outside, "I'll take you to the bus. Fifty cents." With a resolve to start the day on a better note I trusted him and got on. As we pulled away an angry looking character rode at us shouting. My moto boy swerved to avoid him but Mr Angry rode alongside gesticulating. He didn't look nice. I guessed it was a squabble over territory as after a hundred yards he turned back. We went through the village and out onto the main road, it seemed a long way to the bus stop and I started to consider that I might have been had again. We pulled up outside a primary school. My moto boy switched off his bike and settled down to wait with me. I reckoned that while he waited I was somehow assured that the bus was coming this way. Six thirty came and went; the kids were arriving for school at seven fifteen when I started to question my judgement. Moto boy assured me that it would be here any minute and then it was coming down the road. Tearing in front was Mr Nasty. He pulled up and started pushing my moto boy about. The bus door opened and I went to get on but Mr Nasty was throwing his fat body about and shoved the conductor out the way. He stood in front of me ranting "One hundred and fifty thousand!" Here we go again I thought. This was the scam, the moto boy gets a small slice of the fare, I could live with that but Mr Nasty was after a big one. Resisting the temptation to thump him but not quite able to offer unconditional love I quietly told him to fuck off. "One hundred and fifty thousand!" he snarled, waving a ticket. I gave the conductor seventy-five, it was still way over the top and then pushed past. Mr Nasty started on the conductor but I was in my seat and I wasn't going to pay anymore or get off. We started to move; Nasty shouted his price again, his thin little moustache twitching with rage. I mouthed fuck off, smiled and waved. I was bubbling with adrenalin. Nasty followed the bus for a kilometre or so and then he was gone. The road hairpinned back and forth up the steep hill away from the lake. There was at last some forest to see. Though it was by no means pristine it helped to take my mind off the confrontation. Sitting next to me on the bench seat was a handsome boy of about fifteen and his dad. The boy grinned continuously and I guessed he was challenged in some way. He offered me his camera as a gift, its lens was broken but he'd snapped some nice pictures he wanted me to have, he gestured that they were inside. I looked through the viewfinder and agreed that they were beautiful and mimed that he should look after them. He at least knew he was in heaven. His dad reached over and gave me a small poster advertising his church. It was Roman Catholic somewhere in Da Lat. He pointed to the mass timings and mimed that I must keep this at least. It was a Technicolor Mary and Jesus in abundant green woodland with lambs. It was another heaven.

49 No Baps

I confounded the moto boys by walking the three kilometres into Da Lat town from the bus station. It was a last gesture of defiance and rinsed the away the bad thoughts I was still harbouring for Mr Nasty. By the time I walked back into tourist land it was gone and all that remained was the desire for a good breakfast and clean sheets. So here was the 'Jewel'. It had a nice example of a town park with motorised swan boats on the lake, a shopping complex, golf and scores of hotels; the first westerners since Saigon.

I found what I hoped for, a delicious breakfast and the last room in a lovely little hotel. I hung out the 'do not disturb sign' and flopped. A cool breeze fluttered the net curtains in from the windows that overlooked the terracotta rooftops. I slept for hours in a beautiful old bed with crisp linen.

Refreshed I looked through my maps and guidebooks. I thought maybe I could make a last attempt at a border trip. Da Lat is known for a group of motorbike guides who call themselves the 'Easy Riders'. Though they were bound to be more accustomed to taking tourists round the local sights it said in the book that they'd taken tourists all the way up to Hanoi.

Below Yok Don and above Cat Tien National Parks Vietnam Route Fourteen runs along the border with Mondulkiri in Cambodia, there's a road crossing at Dak Dam. It would be a convenient place to bring logs across from the forests on the Cambodian side straight down to Saigon. I went out to find my rider.

The obvious place to be found by a guide is in one of the tourist bars and cafés. I wandered over to one close to the hotel ordered a coffee with tinned milk and waited. Across from me were a bunch of gap year travellers, a mixture of American and European grunge kids. It was as if the old conspiracy theories had been handed on in a long relay of hippy runners. They even used 'Yeh' and 'Man' in the same sentence. There were conspiracies on dope and oil, the snooping government, the usual. What struck me though was the lack of conviction in their deliveries. I wasn't judging; I could have been one of those kids. I've spouted much the same for the last thirty years off and on. But like them I've never really believed that I could be one of the tortured or the oppressed – starving or poor. Fascist dictators happen elsewhere. Only drongos join the army to fight in foreign wars. I guess it's a kind of therapy. It can't be about reality because those who do believe their own hype are branded as fanatics or deluded. We avoid them.

Thankfully before I became the frightening prophet of the apocalypse, the really scary type that believes it and gate crashed their table I was saved. "I'm an Easy Rider, are you thinking of taking a tour?" He was a craggy looking guy of my age with a distressed leather flying-jacket. He looked the part. I told him where I wanted to go. He laughed, "No chance, not if you paid me a thousand dollars." It seemed a bit extreme. "Why not?" "Because my friend, the soldiers would confiscate my bike and me and my family would starve." Then in his American biker patois, "Noo-fuckin-way." He smiled and then said "So why don't you let me take you on a tour tomorrow instead?" "No thanks I'm going to rest if I can't do the border run." He gave me an enquiring look, "Anyway, what do you want to go there for?" "Probably for the same reason you won't take me." We grinned and that was that. He went looking for an easier punter.

"I asked for a bloody amburger! An amburger's got bloody bread for fucks sake." The lady who seemed to be cooking and waiting table single-handed apologised "I get you bread, so sorry." "I want a fuckin bap. That's what amburgers ave." We all winced. The very dodgy looking English bloke poked at his meal with a finger. "An the chips, they aint chips." He muttered as his pretty Vietnamese rent boy looked out the window. He'd obviously strayed just too far from long life white bread and lard in pursuit of an exotic screw. We all have a breaking point. And time for me to leave I thought.

It had been the last try, there was to be no trip to the border with a guide. I considered renting a bike and doing it myself but I needed to be prepared to give it more time than I had available to me. I was not going to just turn up on a day trip and catch 'em red handed. Anyway I'd probably be taken for a journalist in search of a story on the montagnards; westerners weren't welcome up by the border at the moment it was clear. However as a European buyer of furniture I would be most appreciated. Before I turned in I surfed the web for factories in Saigon and sent out a mail to half a dozen requesting an appointment.

50 Little Hands

The hotel owners booked me on a bus, which thankfully carried mainly Vietnamese travellers. I wanted to watch the scenery in anonymity. We travelled Route Twenty through uninspiring countryside till we reached the fringes of Cat Thien National park. Up in the high pass where logs would be harder to poach the jungle was gloriously green and dense. It was bursting to take on the road too it was so vigorous. The coach weaved its way through the turns in the road and I swooned like some kid over a pop idol. I wanted to shout 'I love you forest!' As we descended the edges became a bit torn and ragged where the pickings were easier but it was still a pleasure. We passed a small clearing with logs piled up and a cabin standing in the midst. A big new American style land cruiser was parked on the rugged ground. It could have been a photo shoot dressed for the vehicle manufacturer or a tobacco company advert. It was the alluring image of man's triumph over nature, the might of his machinery and the grit in his belly. And of course when the real man rests from his tough work he smokes full flavoured tobacco.

I wondered why we have the notion that the forest is to be conquered and that nature is our adversary. It seems the media is geared towards perpetuating this belief, generating fear rather than wonder. Nature TV is sold with trailers that are surprisingly similar to the ones that sell Hollywood blockbusters. That deep voice we're so accustomed to, the one that renders 'tough' with gravel and snarls 'kill' touts programmes with titles like 'Killing Machines' or 'Dark Predators'. I wonder how much footage has been devoted to the dangers of sharks yet man kills something like 50 million or more every year pushing them ever closer towards extinction. With such bad publicity who cares if they survive?

Then there's the jungle. It's a dark and dangerous place full of creatures that slither, bite or transmit diseases. It's where savages live, ungodly and evil. We revere the open-faced pioneers that clear the unruly creation for the family of man. Make us safe from the dangerous beasts to live an ordered life of domestication. If we must have forest then plant it in rows.

We made our first stop. It was breakfast time but I'd had a beautiful meal at the hotel so I was content to drink tea and people watch. A kindly looking American in his late fifties I guessed, squeezed his obese hulk out of the coach and into café chair. He smiled and treated everyone with great politeness. I liked the look of him and thought I might chat to him later. Then there were the two girls who had sat opposite me on the coach. They avoided the sun like a death ray. Their skins were milky white and semi-lucent but they looked ill. They joined the entourage of a young gangster who held court at a raised table in the corner. He ignored his followers and talked into a mobile phone while they fawned. His hands and neck were adorned with gold and he flicked a key ring that surely opened the door of an expensive vehicle. He smoked a luxury brand – he bought the myth and so did his friends. But he had a thin moustache like Mr Nasty.

The bus tooted and we were back on the road. I'd had my forest treat for the day it seemed as now regimented rows of plantation teak and acacia lined the road. The little town of Dinh Quan could have straddled a lay line, because a giant had marked its path with huge smooth boulders. They stretched out across a flat plain in irregular sizes into the distance. The alignment was quite uncanny. If the giant had the imagination to point it out though, us lesser beings had shown very little by building a petrol station right up against one of his remarkable markers. The universal petrol station design at that, a slab of flat square metal for a shelter with a garish logo. Why doesn't anyone ever question that hideous design? It's the same the world over. In rural England the planning department will challenge the use of the wrong hinge on a medieval window yet in the same village will consent to the oil company's homogenous design and signage, bright enough to be visible from space on a clear night.

Route Twenty joined Route One and I started to recognise some of the landmarks. I'd been on this road three years previous. We stopped for petrol and I knew I'd stretched my legs here before. The kindly American squeezed out too. He said howdy and extending a hand asked, "Where you been?" I told him I'd been up to the Central Highlands and now I was on my way back to Cambodia. "Now there's a place I haven't been to in a long time. I was in Siem Reap in sixty-three. Yep it was a cowboy town then but it was clean as a whistle." "Where are you going?" I asked. "Well I'll be heading home soon but I'm staying with friends up by Da Lat. Gonna stick round for the celebrations on the fifteenth of April." "What's all that about?" "Why that's the anniversary of the day we got our butts kicked outta here!" He wobbled his considerable belly in laughter.

We weren't far from Saigon now and I wondered if we'd stop again for another break. If we'd pulled in at that same petrol station then there was a good chance that we'd stop for food at their regular haunt too. I had some old friends to look up. As we pulled in I recognised the place straight away, the Nha Hang Restaurant. I walked expectantly to the rear where last time we'd found caged gibbons in a scruffy mini zoo. There was some building work going on so maybe they'd scrapped it but there they were in the corner, two males and a female in a separate cage.

Gibbons are fantastic creatures. Whilst travelling in Thailand a few years ago we spent a day with a fantastic couple who had dedicated their retirement to rescuing gibbons. The rapid loss of habitat there combined with the wildlife trade has meant wild communities have been decimated. Adults are killed for their babies to feed the demand for pets, which are often abused because gibbons don't make good housemates. Bill and Pharanee inspired us with their enthusiasm for these most exciting primates. I say exciting because to be among a troupe when they 'go into one' is a fantastic experience. We first heard them trekking in Borneo. Their call starts with a soft 'who, who, who' then builds and builds until it's a mad raucous scream; but that's just the sound track. Standing with Bill and Pharanee we watched how their rescued gibbons behaved. A black male swung from a branch and started the soft call, soon the others, male and female, were swinging in all directions calling softly too. As the intensity of the call increased so did the speed at which they moved through the branches. By the time the screaming pitch was reached there were arms and legs moving in a frenzied blur back and forth. Bunty and I stood in awe and wonder at the joyous display that whizzed above our heads at fantastic speed and volume.

I was both happy and sad to see them for obvious reasons and went to say hello. They were Pileated Gibbons; the males are black with a white ring around the face while the females are a sandy buff colour. The female held out her hand she was used to asking for food. I held out my empty hand ready to withdraw if she was at all spiteful. She gently took hold of a few of my fingers and held them. Her hand so like a small human. I talked to her for a few minutes and all the while she rubbed her thumb along mine; I wasn't sure who was comforting whom. I said hello to the boys. One slapped my hand and started a soft call. I went back out to the front to buy some jackfruit to share. The males were grabby but they weren't bad considering, the female was as gentle as could be. I pulled out the segments of the jackfruit one by one and she carefully took them from my hand. We polished off two big fruits. I went to check that the bus wasn't going to leave without me and was happy to see that the driver had just got his meal. We had plenty of time. The ladies selling fruit outside were cheerful to see me coming back for more and I guessed they knew I was sharing it because they gave me extra too. I split the fruit three ways and watched them devour it. Then just for me it seemed they went into one, flying and screaming about using every inch of the restricted space. I would have loved to put them back in a forest safe from the humans.

I sat and talked till the bus tooted. The boys and I touched hands and then I said good-bye to their sister. We held hands and took a long look into each other's eyes. There were no promises I could keep; there was nothing to say.

51 Tree in a Basket

The Northern outskirts of Saigon are streaked with tributaries to the Saigon River that flows into the South China Sea. I kept my eye open for any sign of the logging trade around the wharfs and container ports along the way. For a moment I mistook the tangled giant as something to do with the Theme Park that had been signposted for the last few kilometres. As the coach got close though I could see that it was a rainforest tree, a parasitical Fig still green with foliage maybe twenty feet tall in a big basket. It was a garden centre selling jungle plant life. Behind were their deceased relatives in a big pile; round logs stacked high enough to be visible above the tall fences. I decided to come back later to investigate.

We crossed the Saigon River past a little kitsch Eiffel Tower that stands on the corner and drove along by the old French Basin Dock Yard; it appears to have stood the test of time as a working design. Though its waterfront location and colonial architecture will no doubt ensure that if the money keeps rolling in it will be loft apartments before long. I checked into a hotel recommended by the lady at Dreams in Dal Lat, dumped my bags and got a moto back out onto Route One. The Suoi Tien Park being right next door to the log pile was the obvious route to go and take a look round. The moto dropped me outside the theme park and I went in. It was all Chinese and

Vietnamese fables written large with brightly painted dragons, gods and mythology. It would have been fun on another day but I was looking for a high vantage point to take a look at the logs in the compound next door. There was nothing close enough.

I found my moto and asked him to ride just a bit further. We stopped outside the mill where the logs were stacked. There was no one on the gate so I walked in. There was maybe a couple hundred hardwood logs stacked around a machine mill. I laid my hands on them, I wondered if the spirits had come with them to wait. I just felt sad. I sensed no trace of the forest energy; they were carcases beside the roar of the motorway. I was ready to pick a fight and defiantly took pictures willing someone to try and stop me. I guy came out from the mill and stared but went back to his work.

Back out on the road I looked at the living trees in wicker bins ready to be shipped to a wealthy garden somewhere. I thought perhaps it would be the supreme irony that maybe someone made rich from destroying the forest might buy one of these for their garden. Perhaps they'd have a Gibbon for a pet too.

I checked my mail for anything from furniture companies. Of the half a dozen requests I'd sent requesting a meeting I'd only received one reply. It was a start though and although it was past office hours I sent a confirmation that I would visit them in the morning. I had a flight booked back to Phnom Penh the following night, Visa on arrival. I hadn't wanted to waste valuable time with hanging round the embassy for a stamp or a time consuming overland journey. I had just three days till my departure back to the UK from Cambodia, only one more in Vietnam to wrap up what I came here to do.

I enjoyed my last evening walking around the streets soaking up the sights. I had a great dish of Com Chay and popped into the little shop next door to the hotel for bargain price water and a couple of cans of beer to watch a bit of fuzzy TV before crashing. I was tired and mistakenly gave the shopkeeper a fifty thousand dong note for a fifty. He waved it in my face, "You must be careful, this is fifty thousand!" "Thanks, you're a kind and honest man." I said squeezing his arm. It was a warm note to end the day.

Up bright and early to make the most of the day I sat for breakfast in the hotel lobby that doubled as an overnight garage. The heavily lacquered low table was set up amongst the step-through's and the family hatchback. It took me back to childhood memories of my father who worked as a chauffeur. His daytime quarters were the garages, which he'd brightened up with cast-offs from the big house. I pictured him sitting in faded grandeur eating one of the thick sandwiches my mother used to make, the smell of oil and polished chrome, a big grin on his face.

The hotel owner helped me fix up a taxi to take me out to the Industrial area in Bihn Duong Province where the Hiep Long furniture company have their factory. The driver spoke very minimal English so she explained where I wanted to go before we set off. We arrived in the area but the modern Industrial Zones were as featureless as they are the world over and the driver cruised back and forth looking for the street. We had to be close because I saw signs for other furniture manufacturing factories around including one that I'd emailed. A guard at one of the gates gave us good directions and we turned into a lane off the highway as the workers' morning break had just started. It was packed with cheerful looking workers spilling into the lane.

The director's deputy received me at reception. He had only just picked up my mail and explained that if I would like to come back later the Director would be happy to see me then. I explained I had a flight to catch and if he could show me what I wanted to see then that would be fine. I outlined my plans to retail garden furniture and asked about the company's product lines and sources. We set off on a tour of the factory and showroom and I got the company profile as we walked. They specialised in garden furniture sourcing their logs from Malaysia, Myanmar and Vietnam. The company employed four hundred and fifty and they had another factory in Saigon itself.

This time I was prepared; I had no illusions of a cottage industry. I expected an industrial operation. It looked similar to the factory in Pleiku. I asked about output. "We export fifteen containers of forty feet a month." "Do you have customers in the UK?" "Yes we have customers there." "Who are they?" "Oh, I can't tell you that." He said looking a bit wary. Fifteen containers a month didn't seem plausible compared with Duc Long's eighty but I decided not to question it now. He showed me their main production line which again was small teams doing repetitive tasks mainly with powered hand tools. At every station, stacked in neat piles of red wood was a set of identical components ready to be assembled further on down the line. "Do you pack in consumer ready packaging?" I wanted to see if there was anything branded. "Yes, I will show you that facility." We left the production hall to the final packaging area. It seemed like much of this days finished production was going into boxes branded 'The Secret Garden Range, by Tropicdane.' We went back to the office and after going through the pretence of enquiring about shipping and terms of business I thanked them for their time and left.

They had made no claims about FSC or sustainable sourcing. Nope they were open that a major source was Myanmar one of the most brutal and repressive regimes in the world. I pondered the possibility that a warning label like the ones they put on cigarette packets might have the same negligible effect. 'This furniture kills, protect the unborn child from your consumer habit.' My new hard skin was making me cynical for sure.

Outside I found my driver and as we made our way back out to the road I asked if we could see another factory. He got the gist of my English though not the detail as we drove from one factory to another without me being able to get through that I wanted to see garden furniture made from tropical hardwood. Finally he took me to a manufacturer of bamboo furniture where the manager spoke good English and he was able to point the driver in the right direction.

The Truong Thanh Furniture Corporation has a high wall and tight security on the gate. My driver told the guard I would like to visit. I was shown into the gatehouse manned by another two uniformed guards and asked to wait. The internal phone rang and I was given the receiver. A lady asked who I was and what did I want? I explained that I was a buyer and although I didn't have an appointment asked if it would be possible to see someone? She told me that I would be required to make an official appointment.

I explained that I would be leaving the country later and asked again if it would be at all possible if someone could meet with me. She instructed me to wait.

I looked onto the yard from the control box. There was a sign for 'No Photos' and the tight security was more akin to a secret military installation. A covered lorry pulled up to the gate and after the guard checked the paperwork it was allowed in. The phone rang and the guard acting on instructions waved the taxi through. We were shown to a little garden with a thatched seating area to wait. It looked completely unnatural situated in the midst of the industrial buildings.

A pretty young lady in very western office attire came down to see me. She handed me a welcome bottle of cold water and asked what I'd come to see. I had perfected my western buyer patter now and she offered to show me the company's range. We went up to the showroom. It looked like somebody's attempt at creating a tropical island set in a concrete multi-storey car park. There were the familiar designs of loungers, tables and chairs; I tried to look excited but there seemed little to distinguish one manufacturer from another. We sat under another thatch to talk business.

As if to sort the men from the boys she informed me that for a first purchase I would be required to make a minimum order of five container loads. I raised my eyebrows and she qualified it by saying perhaps in the low season two to three would be acceptable. I remarked on the different types of wood used in the different ranges to prompt sources. Their brochure said that the vast majority of the source material came from the Highland Provinces of Vietnam. However, she said that their timber came from all over world. She cited Myanmar, Laos, Malaysia and Brazil. "And from Vietnam." I added. "Yes and from Vietnam." I asked about environmental standards. She pointed to the FSC certificate on the wall. I went to take a look. It stated that the company had met the requirements of the FSC for products listed in the attached schedule. It was not attached. It was clear how displaying a certificate for a small proportion of the company's output could lend a green tick to other questionable supplies. "So how many containers do you ship a month?" "The company exports between seventy and eighty containers a month." She said. "That's a lot of furniture!" I said, doing some more mental arithmetic. So far I'd only scratched the surface, three companies, but already I'd seen facilities capable of exporting 25,000 table and chair sets a month.

I wanted to get the names of UK companies involved. "I've been thinking that an initial order of five containers will be too big for me. Perhaps if I contacted one of your UK customers they might be prepared to share an order with me?" She wasn't going to go for it and shrugged. "Also I've been thinking that if you supply a customer in my country then they will be selling the same product. This will not be good for me. Can you tell me who your customers are?" "Why you worry about this? If you have already sold to your client then it doesn't matter who else sells the same product. I cannot tell you who our customers are." She was probably a junior exec but she was sharp. I made noises that I'd seen enough but I was hoping that I'd get more of a look around the factory. As we left the showroom I pointed to finished product ready for packaging and said that it looked very beautiful. We went to take a look. I gushed a bit about the modern plant. "Would you like to take look?" "Oh yes please." It was automated with large machines doing much of the work carried out by production teams elsewhere. It was a daunting prospect, acres of factory eating the forest and churning out more anonymous product. Some of the chairs were strung with material seating and it occurred to me that however hardwearing the timber was the life of these pieces would ultimately be determined by the life of the cloth. In our throw away society how many consumers would renew the material once it rotted, or even stained? If a replacement is inexpensive then why bother? It's an excuse to go shopping.

We came to the packing hall; this lot was to be marketed as from the 'Oxford Garden Furniture Company'. How wonderfully honest and solid a name I thought.

DON'T BUY IT

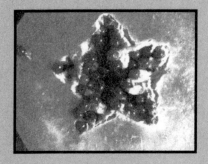

How soon will you realise

that the only thing you don't have

is the direct experience

that there's nothing you need

that you don't have?

Ken Keys JR. (Handbook to higher consciousness)

Happiness is to be found on the inside.
N. Sputnik

52 Don't Buy It

The brothers and sisters were in coffins of brown cardboard packed in a metal container on their way to Europe or the USA. The spirits of the forest headed for a store near you. It would be where the journey ends. I planned to be there when they arrived.

I couldn't get on the flight back to Cambodia quick enough. I needed to be back with people who understood how the anger feels; that wouldn't be sacred of what I had to say, wouldn't feel threatened or defensive.

The chaos of the airport traffic was strangely comforting as my moto weaved its way back into Phnom Penh. It was like coming home. The apartment back on Street 51 was empty, my friend Kerry was working late so I sat out on the balcony and thought about how it would all turn out. For Sek and communities like his, the forest which is their life and the lives that call it home, like the beautiful gibbons I met a couple of days ago; the richness of the tribal cultures up in Ratanakiri hanging by a thread. I felt sad and helpless. But what was new? It's part of our culture to look upon the world and be sad and helpless, it's what we do. It's our coping strategy.

While I was here I had an outlet in the company of Sena or the guys from Global Witness. They knew the score but at home I feared what the reaction to the rant bubbling up inside me would be. I imagined the scenario, "So Ken, tell us all about the trip to Cambodia." "Well, I went to find a Spirit Forest but actually much of it has either been logged, is being burnt or poached and what hasn't is hanging by a thread. And the reason the lives of ancient cultures are being destroyed, precious wildlife is being trashed and the gangsters that got rich on it are getting even wealthier is because we just love to shop." I think it would be a swift move onwards to, "Mmm so Bunty how about the yoga, how did that go?"

But why should it be scary? It's not like I'd be saying you have to give up your car. The truth is that nothing I've seen along the route of my tree, that is causing this destruction is essential. If you make the connection between the furniture in the garden store and the complete annihilation of wildlife and cultures; between a set of garden chairs you'll probably get a few sunny week-ends out of during a British summer and the death of a precious ecosystem, would you buy it? Take the security blanket of fatalism out of the equation and ask yourself is it worth it? Remember poor people don't benefit just gangsters, and corrupt officials. We can't even kid ourselves that we're helping out the worse off.

I started to think about how much of what's precious in this world is being lost because we shop. The aquarium trade, species of fish forced to the edge of extinction for a nice home feature. Coral reefs dynamited and poisoned with Cyanide to feed the live fish market. Rivers that are polluted with mercury in the pursuit of gold and indigenous people who lose their land to mine for shiny things like diamonds and even chrome. The list is frightening. I started to think about the impact of just not buying the things we mostly buy on a whim. It was a positive thought.

In 1999 Global Witness visited twenty companies in Vietnam and estimated that together they were responsible for exporting three hundred and fifty containers packed with hardwood furniture and flooring every month. Four of those companies accounted for nearly half the output but only one exceeded forty containers a month. Four years later I visited three companies chosen pretty much randomly and two of them were exporting seventy to eighty containers a month. It would probably be fair to say that business is booming. Just a modest increase on the 1999 figures would amount to five thousand container loads a year. But what if we just stopped buying it? Think of that stuff that clogs up your garage or shed for ten months of the year as death to forest, animals and people. And you know that you don't need it.

OUTTA HERE

I'd been looking for an encapsulated experience,

one to put things into perspective, the cipher

for the sum of my acquired knowledge, the

conclusion. As I made my preparations to leave I

quietly realised a new beginning.

53 Out of Juice

My last full day in Cambodia was going to be busy. I'd forgotten to reconfirm my flights, perhaps tempting fate to give me another week. I ticked that one off straight away, I was outta here tomorrow it was official. I photocopied all the literature I'd collected in Vietnam for Mike at Global Witness and headed over there to say thanks and goodbye.

The office was busy as usual. Mike had a piece of plywood like a trophy on his desk. "It's from the Kingwood Company. I got a sample from a trade fair in Phnom Penh. It's really ironic; they have the factory so well guarded we've had to fly over the place to see what's going on then a sales rep falls over himself to give me a chunk of what they make. I've got some leads to follow up, it could be promising." The phone rang and he gestured for me to get a coffee or tea. I made myself a cold drink and wandered around the office reception looking at the photos on the wall. It was a catalogue of felled logs, bulldozers, chainsaws and aerial shots of holes in the forest. I studied the big

old maps that stretched nearly up to the ceiling, "They're old American Bombing maps." said Marcos as he walked by. I traced my progress up from Phnom Penh to Preah Vear and Siem Reap, my first trip with Sena and then to Kompong Thma, Sek's home. Then back up North to Ratanakiri an ancient word for Diamond Forest – the one and only gem. All of these places on the old map a reassuring Rain Forest green. When it came off the press in the mid sixties three quarters of Cambodia was covered in primary forest. Today it can't be much more than a tattered twenty-five, thirty percent.

Drawn in hatched blocks like dark clouds over the pieces of the Rain Forest Green that still remained were the boundaries of the logging concessions. The country carved up like a TV dinner, the companies just waiting for the flurry of a pen on a revised development plan or a new deal signed in secret. The destiny of the forests hung on the decisions made by people as remote from the outcome on life on the ground as the US bombing planners of the sixties.

But what if the lines on the map were as living as the lines on a human face. What if those people could feel the wonder of the earth contained in the paper and ink, sense the moisture on a leaf as they touched the shiny paper or hear the flap of a horn bill's wing as the map was gently unrolled. Would they recoil in pain from the bullets and landmines, would they see heaven traced out before them? I held my hands flat to the paper and said a little prayer.

Mike was off the phone but clearly I'd come at a busy time. He smiled but looked harassed. "I'll leave you to the good work. Keep getting in their hair!" I said extending a hand. "Sure, good luck with whatever you choose to do."

I called Sena. I wanted to spend some quality time with him before I left for home. He suggested that I met with him in town as he had some material for me to take back; some pictures and aerial video footage showing military logging camps, their log piles and timber mills, the illegal logging in national parks. Plenty of stuff to get angry about I thought to myself. Then tomorrow I could go to his house before I flew out. He'd take me to the airport. It seemed like a plan.

It was good to see my smiling chum. Sena called at the apartment with his daughter in the car. We sat and chatted briefly about my trip to Vietnam while she bounced on the back seat. "Did you find your tree?" "Who knows? I followed the path." "Did they let you get to the border?" "Nah, it's buttoned up tight." "Ah that's because you didn't have me with you!" We laughed and I

213

acknowledged that it probably would have been a hell of a lot easier with him as my guide. "I think they must be very jumpy at the moment with all the trouble with the Montagnards. I was up there before all that started and they were still very strict. I pretended my moto had broken down to take some pictures at a log rest by the border and the Vietnamese soldiers were very quick to come and see what I was doing. They search my bike but somehow they didn't find the camera." "That's because they were Fukin Stoopid! Anyway I'll see you tomorrow." I said getting out. Noticing a bash in the door and the side mirror hanging off I asked, "What happened to your car?" "Some gangster car drove into me. Somebody was chasing him and he hit my car and then smashed into a wall. He was dead when I got to him." He shrugged and tutted like it was a supermarket scrape. "Stoopid!"

It's the first time on a long trip that with the flight home in sight, I really want to go home. I'd not allowed myself to think too much about home and Bunty but now the barriers were coming down I just wanted to be on my way back. Once I'd done my chores I took a walk out in the late afternoon sunshine to catch it setting down by the river. Kids were playing in the spray of the fountains by the Independence Monument and across the road a small collection of renegade fairground operators had set up outside the main amusement park. One had commandeered a corner lot that had a lovely old tree in the middle. Beneath he'd marked out a track for six ancient mini cars. They had an uncanny resemblance to Noddy's two-seater and for a minute I considered what these would be worth restored in Europe; shaking that out of my head I watched a father and daughter creep round the figure of eight scraped from the weeds. The juice in the battery was all but gone but the wonder on the little girl's face is a lovely memory. It was the sweetness I needed to say goodbye, a dessert for the eyes and heart.

54 Strange Fish

As I got ready to go I looked at the paleness of my skin in the mirror and said to myself "you didn't even get a suntan!" I consoled myself with losing a few pounds to the Alien. I hugged Kerry and thanked her and Frank her partner, for the generosity. I wai'd Pal the house girl for her attentive hospitality and I was gone. Out in the street my regular moto boy was waiting. A row of white teeth flashed beneath his dashing Errol Flynn tash. We were ready to roll. Then with the theme tune to Rawhide building in my head I mounted up and said, "Lets split this crazy town"

I had only one more goodbye. The family had set up a decorated table for lunch in the little courtyard where I'd worn my shoes down dancing on Khmer New Years. Sena's wife dressed in the pyjama set customary for Khmer ladies to wear at the end of day fussed around while his daughter filled the beer glasses with ice. My small gift of fruit and chocolate was returned to the table with the rest of the pre lunch snacks. I emptied my pockets of Riel for the kids and then Sena and I sat and chatted.

"So, I think this was a crazy time for you." I smiled and shook my head in agreement "What will you do now?" "Well obviously I'm looking forward to seeing my wife and my two sons and my grandchildren too." "Oh yes, I forgot you are a grandfather too." "Then I want to finish the journey for the tree too. Maybe find the port where the brothers and sisters from Ratanakiri might have arrived. Some people say that at the old ports of England it's still possible to feel the spirits of the slaves that landed there from Africa. Maybe I'll feel something of my tree too. Whatever, I'm sure I'll know what to do when it comes to it."

"And what's on the CDs?" "There's the pictures I told you about, the military involvement in the logging that's still going on. Also there's a video I took about the wildlife trade. I didn't talk about it because I knew how upset you were about the things you saw at Preah Vear. I hope that you can pass on a copy to the contact I have in England?" "Sure." "It's not for the soft heart. But there are

215

people who sell many animal parts to cure sickness and some to make them sexy. Also some people like to eat bushmeat, monkeys and other animals from the forest." "I just don't understand why people aren't content with pork or chicken." " Also you know when we were up in PBY I found out about a businessman who has been given government contracts to breed monkeys for experiments but first he must catch wild ones. They say he is allowed to catch four hundred to start." "Fuck, that's horrible." "But we must stop this conversation because we are going to eat soon. My wife is only cooking vegetables for you so you don't have to worry. There is a little fish too if you want it. I will be eating some if that's OK for you?" "Of course don't be silly." Our hostess had made an array of vegetable dishes and a dish with cured fish that had a powerful flavour. It reminded me of packet Parmesan somehow. I picked at a bit to be polite.

We talked a little bit about the recent killing of a Trade Union leader; he'd escaped a grenade attack on the rally held by one of the opposition leaders, Sam Rainsey a few years ago. He hadn't been so lucky this time and had been shot down in the street. It was dangerous to be outspoken here despite the veneer of democracy. "Sena, I know you're a survivor but please keep it that way." "It's OK. You know I have a lucky thing like you have your stones. It keeps me safe." "What's that?" "OK I'll tell you. It is customary for the oldest son to be the last one to say goodbye to their parent before the funeral pyre is lit. As the monk lights the fire he quickly takes the shroud from the face and gives it to the son. I have my mother's face to keep me safe." He offered the neatly wrapped cloth for me to see. I touched it without disturbing the folds; like the human lines on a map I thought. "Before I had my mother's face to keep me safe I had an old cloth that a monk gave me. We were hiding together in a cave during the Khmer Rouge times. As my brother, I want you to have it now to keep you safe too." I resisted only momentarily, I was intrigued to see it. I unfolded the aged cloth that had been cut into a triangular shape. There were geometric designs and text written in Sanskrit clearly arranged with purpose. "What does it mean?" "I don't know, the monk said it would keep me safe and it worked didn't it?" "Are you sure you want to give it away?" "Sure, these things are for passing on brother." "Thanks it's a lovely gift. I was going to say I'd really look after 'it' but I suppose it's going to look after me!" We laughed.

After Sena and I had eaten the family came out to sit with us. I had another little play of the 'cheers' game with the little daughter. I thanked his wife again for being kind enough to let Sena be my guide. She smiled and dismissed it in her quiet graceful manner. We lined up for photos in different groups but the time to leave was approaching. We could have just got on his moto to do the kilometre to the airport but Sena decided I was going to get a family send off so our dining table had to be moved to get the car out causing a great palaver. I would of happily slipped away now but I wasn't going to get off lightly.

We lined up by the departure gate; it was another Wizard of Oz farewell. I hugged Sena, kissed and wai'd the rest of them and then tapping my ruby slippers. There's no place like …

KRIME AND MEANIE

Like the jungle and its beautiful struggle to

the light I am also subject to gravity. The

weight of conditioning that awaits the end

of my flight will dull certainty I'm sure. Here

though at the top of the arc and before the

descent things seem clear.

55 Part 1. A Scary Tale

Like the children's fairy tale I kept seeing the King with no clothes; I hoped I could expose his cheating tailors for what they are.

As we climbed out of Phnom Penh airspace I looked back down on heaven. If I accepted the complicated version of the story there were more questions without an answer than I could have ever imagined. I had much to learn according to anybody I asked regarding the simple questions that ran around my head. The obvious one being how come we're allowing the forest to be destroyed?

I'd been going through the 'complicated story' ever since that day in my room recuperating from the alien attack to my gut. After my 'simple reality trip' I couldn't help but see a hairy-arsed monarch riding past every time I pondered the mechanics of the destruction. The way I see it we're in a straightforward bind. We're frightened. When we're frightened we want to be comforted. It's the simplest need for the most basic of human conditions. Yet the comfort we receive is rarely uncomplicated loving kindness. I believe this single instinct and our confused response to it is the driving force behind the destruction of our world.

From our earliest months most of us are weaned off simple loving kindness as a response to our fears. We are introduced to the concepts of punishment and reward. It may be with loving intent but we are trained to suppress our fears with either the greater fear of punishment or with the reward of something pleasant. Before we have the intellect to understand the source of our fears the clarity becomes a fog. As we grow we are encouraged to become empowered and to take responsibility for our own feelings. Naturally we continue to administer our own rewards, for the now indescribable feelings we have inside. We have been conditioned to consume.

We're buried in the avalanche of reasons to be fearful from terrorism to cellulite. We suppressed the real connection to our fears so long ago that we now have a jumble of names to try and describe the empty hall of worry, insecurity, jealousy, anger or uselessness we have inside. But they're just versions of fear. Just as we became empowered to administer our own rewards early on some will develop another strategy. They will start to punish their internal feelings by externalising them. They project power. It has the added bonus of making consumption easier therefore in our confused state considered successful. Ironically powerlessness is something we've added to the fear list along with our fear of failure, even fear of fear. We're easy meat for the Marketers and the terror-peddling politicians.

While we envy the powerful for their access to seemingly unlimited rewards we try and blot out our own fears with the common man's opium, buying stuff. It's a comfort drug and like any addictive substance its efficacy diminishes. We've got to buy more and because we seldom have more money for our habit we've got to buy our drug cheaper. We're hooked on cheap gear.

Our pushers are upping the scale of production to cater for our massive habit daily and are more than happy to lend us the money to sustain us in our hour of need. Like most addicts we like a delusion; that we can't live without it or that someone else is to blame. We especially like a conspiracy theory or a dark corporate plan but what if the figures involved were no more complicated than say a fairy story?

Once upon a time in a land far far away there was a King who ruled a kingdom of forests. It was a happy place where all the animals and birds lived the way god had arranged it. It wasn't because he was a good King he was just too busy playing with his Kingly toys to bother anyone. He used to take very long naps and decided to give all his tedious ruling jobs to Krime Moneyster and all his protecting jobs to Greanie Meanie.

But let's start at the very beginning when both Krime and Greanie were little boys because inside every fairy story there's another one. Once upon a time in two young lives far far away, Krime, a small chubby boy a packet of sweets his only comfort and protection, and Greanie a quiet detachment his shield, stepped alone into the big world - little children confused by the feelings that lived inside.

Their new world of school was as scary as any dark wood from the teacher's stories. They were two little pigs with flimsy houses. Greanie's daddy had chastised him and told him he was stupid whenever he was frightened and now he dreaded the small fluttering bird inside that would reveal his shame; he stayed close to the edge of the playground and out of trouble.

The children laughed at Krime because he was so fat that his trousers shone. Their taunts stung him but he gave the big boys sweets and told them there'd be more if they would be his best friends. His biggest fear was of being without his little packet of bribes.

One day a bully picked on Greanie but one thing his daddy had taught him was how to be quiet while he trembled inside. He held back the tears when the big boy hit him and all the others said he was brave and could be one of their gang any day. It was nearly as good as a snuggle and he liked belonging.

When Krime became a man he saw that just like sweets if you had the things that other people wanted the more they wanted to be your friend. All he needed to do was have more money to get those things. At first he worked hard but soon realised that working hard was not enough, any fool can work and there's seldom any money in it. Stealing was easier. Steal from the rich though and they'll shut you up in the big house. Krime needed another way to get rich because he did so want people to like him.

When Greanie became a man he joined the army, it would be just like being in the gang he thought. He was trained along with the other new recruits in how not to cry out when people are downright nasty to you. He was really good at it and very soon was able to sit in a puddle of cold water for a whole night while his trainer shouted very unpleasant things. Once he had learned these tricks he was taught how to make the 'enemy' cry out and 'give in' by being very mean or spiteful. It was a bit puzzling at times when of course everybody knew that the 'good book' said to be nice but the other recruits were just as confused and Greanie and the boys became the best of friends. When his training was over Greanie saw that people liked his new uniform. They knew that he must be very brave because grown ups loved to tell stories of how fearless our soldiers are. It was quite nice but he really only wanted to be with his friends in the army. They were the only ones who understood the secret; that they wanted to be nice but had been trained to be mean. Nice made you cry and they must be big and strong. Greanie stopped seeing the nice things in his world.

56 Part 2. Dead Enders

The in-flight food started to come round and I left Krime and Greanie for a while. I was being eased back into the amnesia of the West, the small worries, like had my vegetarian meal been requested? Taking my mind off the big one. I was only half an hour out of Phnom Penh and yet I could feel the agitation that I wasn't going to get what I'd ordered. In a way I was happy that I wasn't on the list. Stupid expectations.

Back to the story. So here we have Krime and Meanie much like people you might have met shaped by the strategies that got them through their childhood. If their life so far was as simple as a fairy tale then what becomes of them is no more complicated than a soap opera. Now the kids are asleep who better than your favourite cockney wheeler-dealer from Walford to carry on with the tale. Over to you Frank. "Nice one. Luvely!"

The story goes on... Krime without havin' to look too far sees that there's a nice little profit to be 'ad from mixing business with politics. He's sharp enough to realise that if you add a bit of muscle to your dealings it pays even better. The real revelation for ol' Krime is that stealing from the poor is a piece of piss; the already rich and powerful couldn't give a toss.

Now his old mate Greanie had been getting on with his career too. These days he's meaner than ever. Especially since one of his old comrades nearly 'ad 'im rubbed out a few years back. He don't trust his friends anymore. But then they don't exactly rate him since he had a few of the old class eliminated in revenge. Greanie has traded in friendship for 'respect'. Now he just despises the tin pot outfit he's running, he wants respect and he wants big shooters.

Krime has a deal for him. He tells him about the money to be had from cutting down the forest and how he's in a position to sign the contracts. He needs some muscle and he needs protection. "I'll do all the front of stall business, you just have to make sure that everything runs smooth in the back, if you know what I mean. Remember we're old mates, I won't let you down. I'll make sure you have all the things a man of your stature deserves."

With Greanie behind him Krime can milk the opportunities. His political position becomes unassailable. Dissent is dealt with harshly but Krime keeps the spatters off his suit and smiles for the camera.

Nah then. Krime needs to get that cash rolling ASAP. He's got no intention of taking one of Greanie's rusty old bullets. The quicker he's got him sorted with some nice heavy metal the better. After all, happiness is a new gun.

Enter a new and important character Mr Shiny Culture, the middleman. He's a chip off old Krime's block. He likes all the same stuff, a nice bit of gold here and a tasty Mercedes there. In fact he likes to have both; he's got gold on his Merc where others only have chrome. Poor fuckers!

Krime needs to shift the logs Greanie's men have been cutting down and Mr Shiny knows just how to work it so that everybody stays happy "There's millions in this business my friend," says Shiny thumbing his little book of contacts. This is just the kind of deal that Shiny likes, cheap materials, cheap labour and an understanding bouncer to make sure that nobody spoils the gig. Luvely, and the boys like to deal in cash too.

He didn't get this rich by being on the high street and he wouldn't punt dodgy gear from the boot of his Merc either. Na he's got a man with manners that does all this for him. Shiny calls him Saville Row on account of his nice suit and good breeding. Saville looks nice and respectable and lends all the cheap gear a touch of class. Now there's one thing he knows the punters like these days and that's cheap gear with class. They don't want nothing sordid and they do like it cheap.

Shiny has contacts in all the best gaffs around the world but Saville does all the donkey. Old Shiny won't get his fat fingers all over it, he knows better. Na Saville arranges all the things the punters like these days, little badges and nice wrapping. Interfacing, Saville calls it. Creating a brand you can trust.

All is going sweet, the cash is moving nicely and the proletariat are buying the cheap gear like it'll never run out. Greanie's well happy since he got a whole new arsenal of hardware via one of Shiney's contacts and Krime's larging it up with new villas and nice little girlie imports that do 'im special favours.

So far the story is standard fare and most of us would recognise the scenario. So I wonder why anyone hasn't had the savvy to deal with it? I have to say its because we don't want to.

The reason this disaster continues and becomes 'complicated' is because of what happens next in the story. Rather than say "Oi, Mr Shiny there's blood on your stock and we aint having it." While everybody's being discrete our government turns a blind eye or even actively encourages 'trade'. It's all good business after all and surely we can't meddle in the affairs of a sovereign state.

Then the thing that always screws a good party - happens. Somebody chucks up over the carpet, has a fight or pisses in the neighbour's garden. Or to put it another way, our friends Greanie and Krime have lost it.

Scenario 1. People are starving and dropping like flies, oops! Krime spent all the cash on Dom and Beluga while his minions were too busy trying to get some for themselves to notice. Nobody made sure the Prols were fed. Shit and it's on every channel.

Scenario 2. Krime didn't keep the boys with bullets sweet and cor blimey we've got a Coup on our hands, and it's all over the telly.

Scenario 3. The boys with the bullets got fed up with shooting at cans and started using all the new hardware we sold them on the neighbours, and it's all over the telly.

Now we're in a muddle. We're basically very nice people, we've got some of the most dedicated 'doing good' organisations on our side but they've got an impossible task on their hands because of our craving for cheap gear. We want to make things OK but we don't want to leave half the deal on the table either.

Cut to a Whitehall meeting where the unpleasant situation is brought up as agenda number thirty-seven. "So Minister what are we going to do about this business with Mr Saville? He's been doing us proud and there are still plenty of resources in his neck of the wood, if you'll pardon the pun. He's been a staunch supporter of the party too." "Yes I agree I'm sure we can come up with a solution. The last thing we want is for that vulgar boss of his to go selling it to someone with fewer scruples like the Chinese."

Fudge no. 1. Diplomacy/Carrot: "Maybe we could just give this Krime Moneyster a damn good talking too. Surely he'll realise it's in his own interest. We'll even reward him with loans if they can come up with a development scheme or two, as long as it looks good. Tell him there's aid packages available but he must keep his eye on the ball. And look, tell you what, we'll ship some of the 'doing good boys' in to feed up the sickies. After all we we've still got budget from the surplus on trade." Result: Sick people and the 'doing good boys' are on telly. Business as usual, nice work chaps

Fudge 2. Democracy/Stick: "Krime really hasn't handled this at all well. What say we kick him out altogether? Surely we can find our own monkeys to do a better job, it's only a tin pot country after all? We can go in at dawn bomb the daylights out of them. They'll only be popping back at us with all that old M.O.D. stock Shiny dumped on them. Make sure you get your chaps to rip the stuffing out of the infrastructure; they can pay for a nice refit with oil, logs or whatever they have. And get Shiny back on the case with our new monkeys pronto; we want it back on line ASAP. Oh and I suppose you best send in the 'doing good boys'. We want to be sure that their people understand that this was for freedom." Result: They're on telly, our brave boys fighting for freedom and the 'doing good boys' are tending unfortunate collateral damage. Business as usual, nice work chaps.

Whichever fudge you choose the outcome will be the same if you get a monkey to do a corrupt man's job. Let's be honest we only want a smiling fool to make it look legal, one who will trade the natural wonders of his land for a shiny car, a vulgar palace or two and the handshake from somebody from the top table.

What's happening is nothing more complicated than us being the receivers of stolen goods. It's only dressed up to be complicated so that we don't ask too many sensitive questions. But Mr Shiny knows it aint legit; he'd say, "You know what mate you've got 'victim support' in while the blag's still going down.

Like it. Tell you what, why don't we get our thieves sorted with a bit of that Counselling training? Cut out the middleman! Oh fuck that's me, nah best leave it to the professionals ha ha."

The last page of the story is that we've had it all away. There was a last flurry of business when some scientists pointed out that there might be some useful plant and animal DNA to be saved for future use in the war against human ailments. Once that was all in deep freeze they cleared up the last scraps of the forest and bosh!

Mr Shiny took the opportunity to sell out his share in the business to some wannabe Shiny and he and Mr Saville went off in search of cheap gear elsewhere, "blimey they got prisoners working for nothing in China!" There was no further budget for the first division 'doing good boys' either. It was just left to the ideology bashers now, after their final commodity, minds and souls.

Krime slipped over the border when civil unrest flared up again. It was sparked by food riots following months of drought, 'no forest no rain' and alleged profiteering by corrupt officials. Interim military leader Six Star General Greanie Meanie pledged new elections within two years. "Our country needs a period of stability and strong government that only our patriotic leader can provide," said a military spokesman.

57 Rich Country Poor People

It seems to me that a fairy story goes some way to explaining why the Cambodian experience is one going on all over the world in countries rich with resources but poor in the quality of life. How many times have you asked yourself how is it, that in these countrys, people live on or below the poverty line and are saddled with so much debt? How come the shed-load of loans and aid don't ever seem to lift them out of their sorry state?

We could ask why the good people of the International Monetary Fund can't seem to instruct a fledgling economy on how to keep a country sitting on a lake of oil or abundant diamonds, forest or gold in credit? Why the World Bank lends money to organisations, individuals or governments that have a history of stuffing the money in its pockets. And in the case of Cambodia it would seem appropriate to ask the team of donors who on our behalf dish out the aid, why when you've been ripped off for sixteen billion by a bunch of liars and crooks, would you ever consider giving them another one-point- five billion?

The Banks that operate in these countries are, for all the nice words that go into their names like Development or World or whatever, are out there to lend money. And they'll lend it on the basis of turning a profit of course. It generates a demand for bankable projects like rubber plantations or other development tag proposals like hydroelectric plants. The schemes are lauded as saviours of the poor but in reality poor peoples' lives are disrupted and the wealthy cash in. The country and that includes the poor are saddled with debt for years which often means servicing the loan at the expense of social programmes. In short the rich get richer and the poor, well you guessed it.

And what is poor. It's income below a dollar a day according to the big development institutions. If you're urban poor it's a stinking existence and if you live on impoverished land it's probably just as pitiful. But what if you live in the forest and it provides most of what you'll ever need? Thirty dollars a month probably seems more than adequate. But how would you be measured, living the life of your ancestors in the cathedral of the forest? Answer - dirt poor, and in need of saving from this squalor. Chances are you'd be the just the kind of justification required to log out your forest with a development loan to pay the fat man to do it. He and the government would have to exclude you from your old home of course whilst this important development was underway but it wouldn't be long before you could return and scratch out a living between the neat rows of monoculture dependant on big boss handouts. That's as long as you promise to wave and smile at the kind man in the White Land Cruiser.

When I was up in Ratanakiri, Ian the Canadian guy working in Laos told me that Laotian diplomats were intensely embarrassed at having probably the lowest Gross National Product (GDP) in the region. For them it was a matter of national honour that they did everything in their power to make sure that they weren't looked down upon at the big table. This meant that development was the Holy Grail. Consequently Laos is losing its forest in a continuous convoy to Vietnam on a road built by the Vietnamese government to be paid for in Lao logs. What a nice win win for the Vietnamese timber mafia - lots of free logs and a nice road to haul them out on. Aren't they clever?

So it goes back to the first questions. Make it work if you can? If you cut down the forest where people have lived a sustainable life for centuries in the name of development how does it make them richer?

You give their livelihood and home away for the price of a road that goes somewhere they've lived quite happily without seeing up until now. Then the kind man in the White Land Cruiser says that you can live on the land he just stole from you and you can help him pay back the loan he got to plant rows of cash crop that every now and then become worthless because other stupid men planted too much of the same stuff your boss planted. The rains don't come when they should anymore because you cut the trees but when it does come it washes away the soil and does more damage in monetary terms than you ever got for parting with the forest.

For example, twenty thousand hectares of forest in Ratanakiri was clear-cut to create a palm oil plantation. Four thousand five hundred Jarai people were displaced to produce four hundred jobs, which mainly went to immigrant workers. The justification for this lunacy was to combat the destructive practices of swidden farming and to provide employment for local people.

Annually damage caused by deforestation costs more than five times the revenue collected from the sale of logs and the effects will continue long after the money for timber is forgotten. What's more the debt incurred for the ill-conceived schemes will hang round the neck of the country piling up compound interest and keeping the men in land cruisers happy for the longest time. Aren't they clever?

BLIGHTY

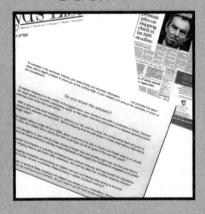

A friend's child had been eyeing me for some months with suspicion. However hard I worked to reassure her that I was her friend she hid behind her mother whenever I was around. Then one day she boldly stepped up to me, she'd worked it out; what it was that had been bothering her. With more of a declaration than a question she said, "You're a space alien aren't you!" I confirmed that I was indeed an alien and after that we got along fine.

Perhaps she was right. This morning I imagined the long hiss of an opening craft door and standing silhouetted in vaporous luminosity.

58 Ming and Von

I was back in old Blighty my feet safely on Sussex soil, well Gatwick carpet to be precise. With a cup of Rosie Lee in sight I screwed it all up by leaving some hand luggage on the plane. I would have to wait until the crew did all the arrival formalities before it would be brought down to the lost luggage desk. I waited in the corner like a lost person.

For an hour or more I watched the British travelling public collect their bags. I cheered myself up by pretending to be an old Germanic Behavioural Psychologist observing my new invention. Ya, following my success with ze rats unt ze maze I have designed the 'revolving belt and treats' for my experiments with humans. "You vill observe zat ven you introduce the subjects to zee experiment they vill display signs of anxiety and vill seek to establish a dominant position. Ah yes here come zee boxes zat contain their treats. They have been trained to take only zee boxes zat have their markings. I have restricted the space so zat the subjects are required to negotiate or to use lower nature stratagems to retrieve their boxes. This often produces conflict between the rats, I mean subjects. I vill always ensure zat at least von subject will not get their box. Observe zee alpha male is assertive at the apex of the belt there, though now I vill change zee dynamics of zee experiment by announcing zat their boxes will now drop onto a different belt. Ah watch them scurry, I love zat bit best!"

So I was back among my fellow consumers and consumed we are by having my space, my case, mine first.

Bunty was through the gate a few hours later and we spent the journey home blurting out our experiences in a random stream of profound and trivial. We continued babbling until we got to the big supermarket. Why we didn't go to the corner shop I don't know. Standing in the cathedral of consumer diversity we were zapped by the white light and multicolour packaging. I looked along the row of twenty odd checkouts, an infinite mirror image of conformity, only their human operators offering any variance. Old ladies with bad perms, a spotty teenager with a love bite and perhaps an embarrassed redundancy victim clad in corporate synthetic work wear swiping the barcodes and avoiding eye contact. We found refuge in the fruit and veg; though much of it's packaged somehow at least a carrot is a carrot and waited till the shock subsided. Everything else had a brand. Why would the baked goods merchandiser consider that twenty different brands of sliced loaf was a good thing? We got round as quickly as possible. As we checked out we got a cheerful kid and she chatted away as she waved our produce over the mirrors and beams of the code reader. The papaya didn't have a label. "Do you know what this is?" she asked. "It's a papaya or paw paw, it's a bit like a mango" Bunty explained. "Is it nice?" "Very you should try it." "Yeh, I will. Definitely" Then she thought for a minute. "You ever had pomegranate?" We nodded yes. "My mate gave me one but I didn't know whether to eat the pips or not?" She was cute and made us smile. I remembered when I started to emerge from my childhood aversion to anything different; I didn't know what to do with the pips on a pomegranate either. I wondered if she would ever experience the fantastic flavour of a perfectly ripe Indian Mango or any of the other real tastes not on the behemoth's shelf? Of all the truly spectacular flavours I've tasted since my friend's mother convinced me to eat fresh parmesan from the little deli that used to serve the Italian community where I grew up; I can't recollect any that came off a supermarket shelf or many that even had a brand, except the cheese perhaps.

In the following weeks I became reclusive. Frustration and anger at what is happening to the forest came in waves. I still hadn't found a way of talking to friends and relatives about the trip and the issues it raised. My initial attempts met with the kind of reaction I had predicted.

I wanted to end the journey and move on. My tree could be on its way so I started to research the possible routes and port of arrival. I'd seen a Hanjin Shipping container at the Pleiku factory so I guessed that would be a start. I checked the shipping schedules and found one originating in Ho Chi Min - bound for

Felixstowe. There would be no way of knowing if it carried any furniture let alone anything made from my tree. My investigation was over now, I already knew the culprits. I would try to be true to my pilgrimage and travel the last miles.

I rode up from Brighton to Felixstowe on my motorbike without a plan. As I left the house I pulled an 'angel card' from the pack. It said, 'Expect a Miracle' I said thanks angels and headed off. Perhaps an opening would present itself.

Dwarfed by the container lorries at the port entrance I picked my way through the gaps and followed the trucks heading in the direction of the cranes. If the harbour I had in mind was a country lane then Felixstowe Container Port is a six-lane motorway. I couldn't see any sign of ships just walls of containers. The trucks pulled into a something like a toll road booth before heading into the stacks of steel boxes forty-foot high. I pulled up on my bike and asked if I could go in too. I knew it was unlikely that they would let me in but I was expecting a miracle. I told them that I belonged to a classic motorbike club and that a container load of old bikes was coming in on the YM Athens from Vietnam. I would like to get some shots for the club website. Their response was encouraging. "You need to go to the police station and ask

for a pass and a 'hi-vis' jacket. If they give you a pass we'll let you in. No probs mate."

I gave the policewoman on the desk my story. "Have you got any paper work?" "I've got the schedule here. It's the YM Athens and it docked at seven this morning." "That's not paperwork love. You have to have paper work for security reasons" "Is there somewhere I can get a photo from outside the port then?" Her reaction was stern, "Absolutely not and if you try and take one, even

outside the port they'll, well…" She didn't finish the sentence as if she didn't like the sound of it herself. I opened my mouth to start on another track but she waved me away and shuffled off into another room. I took another ride around. I saw a sign for the 'Timber Dock' but I couldn't get in there either. I smelt pine on the breeze and I reckoned it wasn't what I was after anyway. I rode to the end of the dock road and got off to stretch my legs and get an idea of what five thousand containers might look like; my estimation of a year's furniture trade.

In front of me were metal containers stacked in blocks five by five, they made a formidable impression. Forty-foot high walls perhaps in rows of ten or fifteen, upwards of five hundred containers I guessed. My mind boggled on five thousand. I used the calculator on my phone to do some reckoning, five thousand containers end to end is nearly thirty eight miles. Containing the equivalent of seven hundred and fifty thousand table and chair sets.

A white police van pulled up. The copper asked what was I doing. "Just stretching my legs." "Well this is private property you know and it's a dangerous environment." I told him about the photos for the website hoping for a miracle, a policeman with a burning passion for classic Ducati's escorting me down to the dock. "All in a days work sir!" But it wasn't happening, instead he advised me about the viewing area just outside the port. "Yes we gave the public a small area to view the vessels so they wouldn't need to come in here. I'm sorry but I don't think you'll get much of a view of the Yang Ming this morning though, she'll be down this end of quay" I headed out.

Next to an old wartime fort, which houses the Felixstowe Museum is a small car park that overlooks the estuary and port. There's a little bit of shingle beach, a hamburger stall housed in an old ten-foot container and fifty yards of paved frontage. It's a place for old people to look at the comings and goings. Mostly they stay in their cars but a milky sunshine had tempted a few out. A minibus from an old folks' residential home was parked on the end and four elderly ladies and a gent in a wheelchair looked out. The driver and the care assistant in the front babbled on about some TV reality show and from time to time turned to talk very slowly and loudly to the occupants. I watched the poor old gent cringe with frustration and then resignation. I looked down to the beach, a couple sat in deck chairs at the water's edge. He had a dodgy cap and binoculars and did all the talking; she had a fluffy white perm and the flask.

All that separates public from the edge of the quay here is a chain link fence and I pondered the contradictions on the security front. It was their little game and I was done with it now. I was pleased that I wasn't the only one to see the flaw though as a guy who joined me said, "That's Bin Laden in a fluffy wig down there. There's a Nuke in the hamper." I love being English sometimes.

59 Mssrs 20 Percent

I'd avoided garden centres. I knew that I would have to go; it was the last step. Somehow it was as I expected, terribly normal. There it was pressed in amongst the mainly tasteless tat that is the UK garden centre. It was marketed as the 'Oxford Garden Range' a coincidence or was it the miracle I was to be expecting? I touched the silly little bench it's red wood that once towered to reach the sun. It was Keruing, from the Dipterocarp family and quite possibly a resin tree and most likely from Laos. My journey had started in Cambodia and ended a ten-minute walk from my home in suburbia, from the truly amazing to the awfully mundane. This was the plausible fate of my remarkable tree. Knocked out so cheap the optional cushions were more expensive. All because we lack the imagination to see it for what it is, a magnificent piece of heaven.

If my tree had mixed with Lao timber then this could easily be a fragment of the sister from the Jewel of forests; if it had been warehoused for more than a season or two then it probably would be Cambodian. But it's a small point now because by the time you read this they could well be cutting down the last of the forest in Ratanakiri. It's an interchangeable set of circumstances. There's a corrupt or puppet government and a Mr Shiny at it right now anywhere there's forest to  grab. And we're the receivers, you and me. We could call on our governments to put an end to it but how many of us have written to our MP in the last couple of years or ever? How many even know the name of his or her representative in parliament? And when we do make ourselves heard by taking to the streets like we did in our millions against the Iraq war, who exactly listened? To be perfectly honest I'm fed up with hearing the empty tosh. Nope it's down to you now.

Chances are today you will shop; you have the freedom to shop. It's power and as the corny line from the film says, 'with power comes great responsibility'. Now I've explained the link between this little bit of furniture and the destruction of the forest, the creatures and other people's lives, and I do mean death; I'm making you responsible for their future. So now you won't be able to buy it will you! Not without being a complete bastard anyway. I'm not saying don't ever buy another item but we cannot take anything at face value. Ask questions; don't scan for a reassuring logo and then just part with your cash, shop with care. Remember there are alternatives often made with love and not sold as commodity. Support them.

The Forest Stewardship Council (FSC) are doing a fantastic job in establishing a standard for responsible and sustainable forestry so that you and I can buy something wooden and know that disruption to precious wildlife was kept to a minimum, it was legal and it actually contributed to the fabric of the country it grew in. You will recognise the FSC logo as a green tree and a tick. When it's physically attached to the article there's a fair chance that it's safe. If you buy FSC the odds are that the timber won't come from outside Europe and North America; the majority of producers in Brazil, Malaysia and Indonesia don't meet the criteria. Tiny Ireland has nearly six times more accredited hectares than Malaysia.

There are plenty who claim to only source from well-maintained plantations, that five trees are planted for every one cut down, that kind of spiel. I truly feel sorry for any companies who do get their timber from such a source, if it exists, for the bad rub but there are too many people making this claim for it to stand up. There simply isn't the capacity. If there were then Indonesian Borneo wouldn't have lost fifty two percent of its forest in six years. Timber buyers it seems are happy to accept a transport document (SKSHH) from their Indonesian supplier as proof of origin. These documents are freely available on the black market. In Laos the whole shebang is run by the military so there's no desire for sustainability just hard cash and guns.

So how do you know if its dodgy or not? What about asking an expert, your intuition. If the likes of Mr Shiny came up to you in a pub and said, "How do you fancy some of this garden furniture? It's made of tropical 'ard wood mind. Tell you what, table and chairs an undred an fifty nicker the lot. I'll even fro in a brolly." Think about it. Shiny is bound to be taking at least fifty straight off the top, so that's 'a wonna it owes im' as he would say. Transport it from the pub to Felixstowe and ship it to Singapore. From Singapore change ships and send it on a feeder vessel to Ho Chi Minh City. Then spend some man-hours milling it, shaping it and assembling it. It will have been hauled from the forests of a neighbouring country and officials paid off all along the way. Just imagine what it would cost you to send the parcel alone then add the profit that the manufacturer put on it. Common sense would say the tree was nicked.

Or and this is where it gets scary, huge economies of scale make it possible. The Danish owned 'Susan Maersk', is the largest container ship in the world. It can carry six thousand six hundred, twenty-foot containers. The ship is known as 'post-panamax,' meaning it's too big to fit through the Panama Canal. The 'Susan' typically carries wood pulp, chemicals, machinery, computer parts, furniture, toys and other items on a circular route from China to Europe. "Expect to see more of her ilk in the 21st century", said a Maersk spokesman. "Economies of scale are the key in liner shipping. We've got to put through more volumes to make it more profitable."

It was reported in September 2004 that the world's shipping companies were on a shopping spree for new vessels. It's estimated that global container fleet capacity will grow a staggering fifty percent by 2007. This ramp of growth is set to become a wall that the forest, all its beautiful creatures and people will be up against. The destruction is linked. According to Greenpeace, every two seconds commercial logging trashes ancient forest the size of a football pitch.

The United Nations says globally, the 20% of the world's people in the highest-income countries account for 86% of total private consumption.

So we bear the responsibility but we also hold the key. We're the twenty percent that can bring about the change. It's happening in our lifetime, it's you and me here and now. There's no future solution, it simply won't be there for our grandchildren. Something precious is dying right now before our eyes.

We must at least do nothing! It won't be easy but this is an appeal that requires you to give nothing of your time or wealth. Care deeply; leave your money in the bank for your old age and help save the planet.

Never has it been so important to exercise this choice. Live life as a heaven born child; please don't buy the things you don't need.

Epilogue

The channels that have been my source of knowledge have become a source of dismay. Today I received a press release from Global Witness. It contained the terrible news that commercial logging has resumed in Cambodia. It truly breaks my heart that they're clearing rare and ancient forests to plant Acacia for MDF board. I cannot think of a more pathetic, mundane and to quote my very good friend "Fukin Stoopid" thing to make from paradise.

It was news that swiftly blew open the door that I was closing on my journey. Closure, it's a luxury that we've been led to believe is ours, to turn another fresh page; to submit hard cold knowledge to warm nostalgia.

I already had a vision as to how to close the door for you - Of Sena bumping down a dusty road, his camera and GPS in hand tirelessly facing the seemingly irresistible forces of destruction and the ugly corruption that makes it possible. Recognition too of our friendship and my privilege for the little bit of life's journey we shared together. It was a golden sunset and I felt the warmth on my hand as I pushed the old wood to.

Now the sound of chainsaws and the smell of petrol are on the wind that whips through the gap like a cold snap. Sena is out there now for sure but there's no closure for him. It's slog and my deep admiration for those like Sena is the only warmth I can offer. The people responsible for cutting down Botum Sakor National Park right now would turn tiger to mince for cheap burger. He cannot rest and we cannot shut the door on people like Sek Cheng the resin tapper from Kompong Thma. I'm haunted by his plea,

"Please help us, our situation is desperate."

Also by Eye Books

Riding the Outlaw Trail - Simon Casson
Following the footsteps of Butch Cassidy and the Sundance Kid,
ISBN: 1 903070 228. Price £9.99.

Desert Governess - Phyllis Ellis
A former Benny Hill actress, as governess to the Saudi Arabian
Royal family.
ISBN: 1 903070 015. Price £9.99.

Last of the Nomads - W. J. Peasley
The story of he last desert nomads to live permanently in the
traditional way.
ISBN: 1 903070 325. Price £9.99.

All Will Be Well - Michael Meegan
Stories of love and compassion.
ISBN: 1 903070 279. Price £9.99.

First Contact - Mark Anstice
A 21st Century Discovery of Cannibals + free award winningn DVD
ISBN: 1 903070 260. Price £9.99.

Further Travellers' Tales From Heaven and Hell -
Best entires to a writing competition.
ISBN: 1 903070 112. Price £9.99.

Special Offa - Bob Bibby
A walk along Offa's Dyke looking at the changes over time.
ISBN: 1 903070 287. Price £9.99.

The Good Life - Dorian Amos
A move from Cornwall to the Yukon in search of the good life.
ISBN: 1 903070 309. Price £9.99.

Baghdad Business School - Heyrick Bond Gunning
Setting up a business in the aftermath of conflict.
ISBN: 1 903070 333. Price £9.99.

Green Oranges on Lion Mountain - Emily Joy
An Accidental Optimist working in sierra Leone.
ISBN: 1 903070 295. Price £9.99.

The Con Artist Handbook - Joel Levy
Get wise with The Con.
ISBN: 1 903070 341. Price £9.99.

The Forensics Handbook - Pete Moore
A clear introduction to the life of Forensics.
ISBN: 1 903070 35X. Price £9.99.

Seeking Sanctuary - Hilda Reilly
Western Muslim converts who have chosen Sudan as their home.
ISBN: 1 903070 392. Price £9.99

Lost Lands Forgotten Stories - Alexandra Pratt
20th Century female explorer follows her 19th Century equivalent
ISBN: 1 903070 368. Price £9.99

Jasmine and Arnica - Nicola Naylor
A blind woman's journey around India.
ISBN: 1 903070 171. Price £9.99.

Touching Tibet - Niema Ash
A journey into the heart of this intriguing forbidden kingdom.
ISBN: 1 903070 18X. Price £9.99.

Behind the Veil - Lydia Laube
A shocking account of a nurses Arabian nightmare.
ISBN: 1 903070 198. Price £9.99.

Walking Away - Charlotte Metcalf
A well known film makers African journal.
ISBN: 1 903070 201. Price £9.99.

Travels in Outback Australia - Andrew Stevenson
In search of the original Australians - the Aboriginal People.
ISBN: 1 903070 147. Price £9.99

The European Job - Jonathan Booth
10,000 miles around Europe in a 25 year old classic car.
ISBN: 1 903070 252. Price £9.99

Around the World with 1000 Birds - Russell Boyman
An extraordinary answer to a mid-life crisis.
ISBN: 1 903070 163. Price £9.99

Cry from the Highest Mountain - Tess Burrows
A climb to the point furthest from the centre of the earth.
ISBN: 1 903070 120. Price £9.99

Dancing with Sabrina - Bob Bibby
A journey from source to sea of the River Severn.
ISBN: 1 903070 244. Price £9.99

Grey Paes and Bacon - Bob Bibby
A journey around the canals of the Black Country
ISBN: 1 903070 066. Price £7.99

Jungle Janes - Peter Burden
Twelve middle-aged women take on the Jungle. As seen on Ch 4.
ISBN: 1 903070 05 8. Price £7.99

Travels with my Daughter - Niema Ash
Forget convention, follow your instincts.
ISBN: 1 903070 04 X. Price £7.99

Riding with Ghosts - Gwen Maka
One woman's solo cycle ride from Seattle to Mexico.
ISBN: 1 903070 00 7. Price £7.99

Riding with Ghosts: South of the Border - Gwen Maka
The second part of Gwen's epic cycle trip across the Americas.
ISBN: 1 903070 09 0. Price £7.99

Triumph Round the World - Robbie Marshall
He gave up his world for the freedom of the road.
ISBN: 1 903070 08 2. Price £7.99

Fever Trees of Borneo - Mark Eveleigh
A daring expedition through uncharted jungle.
ISBN: 0 953057 56 9. Price £7.99

Discovery Road - Tim Garrett and Andy Brown
Their mission was to mountain bike around the world.
ISBN: 0 953057 53 4. Price £7.99

Frigid Women - Sue and Victoria Riches
The first all-female expedition to the North Pole.
ISBN: 0 953057 52 6. Price £7.99

Jungle Beat - Roy Follows
Fighting Terrorists in Malaya.
ISBN: 0 953057 57 7. Price £7.99

Slow Winter - Alex Hickman
A personal quest against the backdrop of the war-torn Balkans.
ISBN: 0 953057 58 5. Price £7.99

Tea for Two - Polly Benge
She cycled around India to test her love.
ISBN: 0 953057 59 3. Price £7.99

Traveller's Tales from Heaven and Hell - Various
A collection of short stories from a nationwide competition.
ISBN: 0 953057 51 8. Price £6.99

More Traveller's Tales from Heaven and Hell - Various
The second collection of short stories.
ISBN: 1 903070 02 3. Price £6.99

A Trail of Visions: Route 1 - Vicki Couchman
A stunning photographic essay.
ISBN: 1 871349 338. Price £14.99

A Trail of Visions: Route 2 - Vicki Couchman
The second stunning photographic essay.
ISBN: 0 953057 50 X. Price £16.99